# HOA BOARDS

## What You Need to Know —
## But Weren't Told

CAPTAIN BILL TRAVIS

HOA BOARDS
What You Need to Know — But Weren't Told

Published by Trabide Publications
Gilbert, AZ
Email: BillTravis1@cox.net

Library of Congress Control Number: 2013934338

ISBN 978-0-9890937-6-7 Softcover book edition
ISBN 978-0-9890937-7-4 Mobi eBook edition
ISBN 978-0-9890937-8-1 ePub eBook edition

Cover Design: Jason Orr, Jera Publishing
Interior Design: Stephanie Anderson, Jera Publishing
Back Cover Photo: Connie White, CWLife.con

Interior Photos: BigstockPhoto.com
Authors' Photo: Connie White, CWLife.com

Published in the United States of America

# About the Author

Bill Travis has a combined fifteen years' experience as an HOA board member, and has served in every officer capacity, including Secretary, Treasurer, Vice President, and President. He has been a member of the Board of Directors of an HOA sub-association in Arizona for twelve years, and has served on an HOA master association for three years.

He currently serves as Secretary on the sub-association where he previously served as president for three years, and he serves as a director at large on the master association.

In addition to the fifteen years as an HOA director, he served on the Board of Directors of the International Special Events Society in San Francisco for three years and on a Toastmasters Board of Directors in California for four years; he has a grand total of twenty-two years' experience as a board member.

He was a member of the National Association of Parliamentarians for two years prior to dropping the membership because of his workload.

Bill had a career as an international airline pilot for 35 years. He flew for Pan Am for 28 of those years where he started out as a Flight Engineer, and as seniority allowed, he moved up to First Officer (Co-Pilot), then became an instructor/check pilot on the Boeing 707 where he instructed pilots who were upgrading to that aircraft, and also performed semi-annual check rides (proficiency checks) for pilots as their check and training dates came due.

Later he flew the Boeing 747, and flew as Captain on the Airbus A300 and A310 prior to retiring from aviation in 1991.

In 2013 he wrote and self-published a book titled, "Pan Am Captain, Aiming High" *(available at Amazon.com)*. The book contains a memoir, a brief history of Pan Am, some of his flying experiences, and is also a motivational book dealing with goal setting and visualization.

He is a Real Estate Broker and owns his own brokerage, Captain Bill Realty, LLC in Arizona. However, he has retired from working with clients. Today, he only uses his real estate license to buy and sell houses that he rehabs. He began rehabbing houses in California in 1974 and continues to periodically do rehabbing in Arizona.

While serving on HOA boards, he became educated in HOA operation by attending classes hosted at local colleges, and reading what books were available on the subject. He realized that many associations do not provide board member training and don't make an effort to have board members get educated in HOA operations. Consequently, many board members do not sufficiently understand their HOA's governing documents or the Arizona Statutes that govern non-profit corporations and planned communities, though they should have a working knowledge of both.

The lack of knowledge of the state laws, governing documents, parliamentary procedure and meeting decorum is one cause of so much conflict on boards, and between HOA boards and their association members. Some instructors of HOA classes believe the problems of runaway boards and rogue directors could be eliminated if all directors were required to have some education in HOA operation.

There is a lot of information available on the internet, on HOA attorney websites, and in a few HOA books, but there doesn't seem to be a comprehensive study guide dealing in depth with the subjects that directors should know, that can also be used as an instruction and reference book. Consequently, Bill decided to write this book with the hope that directors who read it will become better board members.

# OTHER BOOKS
## BY CAPTAIN BILL TRAVIS

**Pan Am Captain, Aiming High,**
available on Amazon.com

# BOOK REVIEWS

This is a must read for every director serving on the Board of an Arizona Home Owners Association. HOA conflicts are emotional — they involve our homes and neighbors — therefore, we treat those subjects with significant importance in our everyday life. This book presents several compelling subjects, but most importantly, it takes us on a tour of effective listening and compromise skills. Those skills can help us to navigate through emotionally laden rough waters. The book is also a comprehensive guide to the technicalities of serving as a director on an HOA board.

> **Jonathan Olcott, Esq.**
> Philip Brown | Jonathan Olcott, PLLC
> Phoenix, AZ

Having served on a Board of Directors of a Home Owners Association for over 20 years, I have held every position at some point during my tenure on the Board, and headed up numerous committees. I have served with Bill Travis for more than 10 years and found his knowledge and insight to be invaluable. He has managed to bring his years of experience together in this book to provide his readers with the framework for becoming a Director and serving on an HOA Board. Anyone who currently serves on a Board will find reading this book a necessity and great resource material.

> **Jim Speer**
> HOA Board President

As a former HOA board member, so many of the sections of this guide ring true to me. The director position is fraught with risk and liability, but only when a board is either uneducated or distracted. I had the pleasure of serving with many competent board members, and realize what a plus that is. I'd recommend to any HOA board member taking this guide and devouring it as soon as possible after election. It will be your friend and counselor.

**Marci Johnson**
Business Owner and Former HOA Board Member

As a Home owner and working with the HOA at times, this book is Eye opening. It's surprising how much info is in this book, and how important it is to have this knowledge to properly make decisions for the entire community. Makes you appreciate what our board members have to deal with. This also shows me how important it is to know who you're voting for. I recommend all homeowners read this book to better educate yourself before making complaints.

**Bill Freitag**
Homeowner

Whether you are lobbying for change or want to serve on your Home Owner Association board of directors, this book is a must read. It's rich in content and its' resources provide a great understanding as to the hierarchy of state laws and their relationship with the HOA's CC&R's, and how those relationships affect a board members ability to serve and make educated decisions. As a Realtor for 22 years I see a push-pull relationship between homeowners and HOA boards. Many conflicts could be resolved by both parties taking a greater interest in their understanding of the laws and community rules. This book is a well written educational piece that can be read cover to cover, or can be used for a law or subject specific resource.

**Kristine Devine**
Realty One Group
602-920-7653
Gilbert, AZ

# CONTENTS

# INTRODUCTION

In 2006, a neighbor approached me, stating that he felt the gated community in which we live was not being maintained sufficiently. I had also noticed some areas I felt needed a little TLC, so we took a tour of the community's common property together. On the walk-through, we observed a lot of deferred maintenance; subsequently, we decided to run for the board so we could contribute our input and help the board take care of the deferred maintenance and develop a plan to keep the assets properly maintained in the future.

I quickly learned that being a member of an HOA board requires more than just showing up at meetings to make decisions. It requires understanding the governing documents of the association and having a working knowledge of the laws that govern planned communities. This knowledge is required in order to understand how the HOA should operate within the law, and how board members can avoid personal financial risk. At that time, I didn't know what the CC&R's were, and since there was no training available through the association, I knew I needed an education in HOA operation.

This association had a professional management company managing the business affairs of the association, such as collecting dues, inspecting for resident yard and common property maintenance, hiring vendors to maintain the association assets, and paying the monthly bills. However, it was evident by the deferred maintenance that the management company was not doing a good job. Whose fault was that? One of the first things I learned is that it is the board's responsibility to supervise all agents and employees to see that their jobs are properly performed, and that "*the buck stops with the board.*" I also learned that directors who do not perform their duties properly can put themselves at personal financial risk. Therefore, I felt it was imperative to educate myself. In 2006, there was a series of HOA classes held at a local community college that cost $25 per class, so my neighbor and I began attending them. Today there are more classes available and most are free, as they're sponsored and taught by HOA attorneys who get publicity by meeting board members through these classes.

The classes are an excellent starting point for new directors, as the beginning classes point out what they need to study in order to become better board members. But it requires some woodshedding on the part of the board member.

One excellent side benefit of those classes is that one is able to ask the attorneys questions about various aspects of HOA law when attending the classes, at no cost.

This book will guide you through the Arizona laws and the standard association governing documents that a director should be familiar with

in order to make decisions that comply with these two basic sets of rules and laws. There is also a section on Robert's Rules of Order.

The book can be used as a study guide, where you can read from the front of the book and learn what you need to study further, or as a reference book. It isn't necessary to memorize everything, but you should have a working knowledge of state law and association documents in order to know where to find answers to questions that will arise periodically during HOA board meetings.

In order to challenge you to use your research skills, there is list of questions in the back of the book. You can check out those questions at any time.

This book will also be valuable to homeowners either contemplating buying into a planned community (HOA) or already living in one and desiring to learn more about how the board and the association should operate.

## DISCLAIMER

I am not an attorney, and do not offer legal advice. Please do not interpret anything you read in this book as intending to provide legal advice. For answers to legal questions, and for legal opinions, one should always consult an attorney who is experienced in, and has a good reputation in, the HOA industry.

CHAPTER 1

# WHERE TO START

Congratulations! By buying this book, you've taken the first step to becoming a better educated HOA board member. But there is so much to learn, you may be wondering: "Just where should I begin?"

Well, in order to see the beginning, we'll first take a look at the big picture. Beginning with Chapter 2, "What Is an HOA," this book will lead you through a natural progression of study where you'll learn about the:

- Hierarchy of an association,
- Governing documents of the association,
- State laws that govern planned communities,
- Directors' duties,
- Conducting meetings,
- Robert's Rules of Order,
- Finances,
- Maintenance, and
- Advisors.
- Plus there are a couple of very educational case studies at the end. If you're a new board member, don't read the case studies yet. Save them until after you've become familiar with the non-profit corporation and planned community laws.

There is a ton of information strategically organized in the book to help you learn almost everything you need to know. When you complete this book, you may decide to continue your studies by attending seminars on HOA operation where there is always something new to learn.

# Fast Track

You can begin at the beginning of the book and go straight through, or if you're an experienced HOA director with a working knowledge of the laws and governing documents, you can use the book as a reference guide and go directly to sections that are of current interest to you.

But, as a new board member, you may ask, *"what should I study that will get me up to speed quickly?"* That's an excellent question and here's the answer:

### Duties
First, you need to know the powers and duties of the board, and the duties of directors and officers. That's of paramount importance.

- Go to Chapter 3, "HOA Governing Documents" and read the Bylaws section.
- Next, go to Chapter 5, "Directors and Offices Duties" and study that.
- Finally, go to your own association Bylaws and study them.

### Meeting Decorum
Your association should have adopted some form of parliamentary procedure for meetings. It could be Robert's Rules of Order, or some other format, but the association should have a defined set of rules that every board member can become familiar with. Every meeting should be conducted using those rules so meetings don't end up in chaos, with directors making up rules as they go along. The chairman should make an effort

to have every director become educated in the form of parliamentary procedure the association has adopted.

- Go to Chapter 7, "Conducting Meetings" and read the entire chapter; it's only about seven pages long.
- Pay particular attention to the Meeting Decorum section and the Active Listening subsection.
- Find out what parliamentary procedures your association has adopted and learn them.

### Robert's Rules of Order

Chances are good that your association has adopted Robert's Rules of Order as the parliamentary authority, by notation either in the Bylaws or by Resolution.

- Go to Chapter 8, "Robert's Rules of Order".
- Begin a systematic study of them over a period of time.
- Set a goal of learning them by a certain date by studying a little each day, along with the rest of your director study program.
- You can buy a cheat sheet that has all of the rules on it, or you can make your own and refer to it as necessary.

### Back to the Book

After completing the Fast Track study, you're already prepared to be a good board member.

- You know the directors' and officers' duties.
- You're familiar with conducting business meetings.
- You're familiar with meeting decorum, and
- You're familiar with Robert's Rules of Order.

Now, you're ready to dig in for more serious study!

After the Fast Track study, I suggest starting at the beginning of the book and going straight through. Become thoroughly familiar with Chapter 3, "HOA Governing Documents". That chapter tells you what standard HOA governing documents are, their order of precedence, and what each contains. As you read that chapter, refer to your own governing documents and begin to learn what is in them. You don't need to memorize everything in them; it's more important to know where things are and how to find the answers to questions in the documents as they arise.

After studying the HOA Governing Documents chapter, you're better prepared to study the State Laws chapter. If you're not an Arizona resident, find out where to locate the planned community laws in your state, and study them.

After you complete your study of the governing documents and the laws, you are probably in the top 5% of all directors in the country for HOA board operation knowledge, which means you should be congratulated.

So, congratulations!

After the State Laws chapter, the rest of the book is designed to provide you with more advanced knowledge of how an HOA should be governed. That knowledge will be valuable in working with the rest of the board to keep improving your community while helping to minimize legal risks for the association, the board, and the individual directors.

CHAPTER 2

# What is an HOA?

## HOA Hierarchy

To more fully understand HOA operations, it's necessary to first understand the hierarchy of governance.

### The Laws
The state and federal laws are at the top of the hierarchy. Unless a law specifies that the HOA's Declaration or Bylaws will apply, the law always trumps the HOA's governing documents. If there is any article in the governing documents that conflicts with the law, the law takes precedence.

### The Non-Profit Corporations Act of ARS Title 10 governs all non-profit corporations.

*ARIZONA REVISED STATUES*

Most planned communities are non-profit corporations. If they were not corporations then it would be possible that all homeowners, because of their equal percentage ownership of the common grounds, could have individual liability.

## The Planned Communities Act of ARS Title 33 governs all planned communities.

The Non-Profit Corporations Act in Title 10 and the Planned Communities Act in Title 33 should both be consulted when seeking the answer to a legal question. Since the Planned Communities Act was implemented specifically for planned communities, one should look for an answer there first because in most cases this Act will trump Title 10. However, Title 10 should also be consulted to be certain that it doesn't contain language that would override Title 33. If Title 33 doesn't address a question, then one would proceed to Title 10 to search for the answer.

### HOA Governing Documents

- These are the internal documents that govern an HOA. They are collectively referred to as the "governing documents." They are:
  - Plats;
  - Declaration of Covenants, Conditions and Restrictions (CC&R's);
  - Articles of Incorporation;
  - Bylaws;
  - Rules and Regulations.
- A board of directors governs the association and acts in compliance with the state laws, local ordinances, and the governing documents, as well as any federal laws such as the FHA, ADA, and any others.
- The homeowners elect the board of directors to govern the association.
- Since the homeowners elect the directors, it stands to reason that only the homeowners can remove a director. In the planned community law, there is a specific procedure for homeowners to remove a director.

  Some association Bylaws may have a section providing that a board may declare a director position vacant if a director is absent from three consecutive regularly scheduled meetings.
- The board of directors elects the officers of the board.
- Usually, there are four officers: president, vice president, secretary and treasurer.

- □ Their duties will be spelled out later in Chapter 5, Directors and Officers Duties.
- Directors who are not officers are referred to as "directors at large."
- Directors at large may be assigned to serve on committees or undertake special projects.
- The officers have specific assigned duties for their office, but sometimes those duties are delegated to the management staff, so the officers may also be assigned to serve on committees or undertake special projects.
- The board of directors can remove an officer from the assigned office, after which that person reverts to being a director at large.
- The entire board, as well as each director, has the fiduciary duty to act in the best interest of the association.
- The owners cannot micro-manage the board.
  - □ However, the owners can and should attend meetings, ask questions, and voice their concerns and desires for the community.
- The Bylaws will spell out the powers and duties of the board. They will be discussed in Chapter 5, Directors and Officers Duties.
- The board hires and supervises a community manager to run the daily operation.
  - □ The board makes the policies that the manager must follow.
  - □ The manager hires and supervises his or her staff.
  - □ The board cannot micro-manage the manager or the staff.

# CHAPTER 3

# HOA GOVERNING DOCUMENTS

In this chapter we'll take a look at each of the governing documents in a logical sequence. Later in the chapter we'll list the documents in the order of precedence.

- Articles of Incorporation
- Bylaws
- CC&R's
- Rules and Regulations

## ARTICLES OF INCORPORATION

In Arizona, an association's Articles of Incorporation establish the corporation and its purpose. The Articles are filed with the Arizona Corporate Commission. Future amendments must also be filed with the Commission. The requirements for Articles of Incorporation are found in Title 10 of the ARS, and they include:

- the name of the corporation,
- the corporation address,
- the corporation's purpose,

- the name and address of the association's statutory agent, and
- other information the declarant may wish to include.

The association's true legal name is stated in the Articles of Incorporation. Here is a fictitious name example:

> The name of the corporation is **"The North Side Community Association**," hereinafter referred to as the "Association."

The Articles of Incorporation of each HOA define how the Articles may be amended. Typically, while the Declarant is in control, or before a given period of time, the Articles may be amended by the affirmative vote of 90% of the association members voting. Then after 20 years, they may be amended by the affirmative vote of 75% of the association members voting. By requiring only a percentage of the members voting, amending the articles is a relatively easy task.

## *Duplication*

It isn't uncommon to find an article in the Bylaws duplicated in the Articles of Incorporation or in the CC&R's. Amending the Bylaws is as easy as amending the Articles of Incorporation, however, amending the CC&R's is next to impossible.

When a Board is contemplating amending an article in the Bylaws, it is a good practice to search the Articles of Incorporation and CC&R's for duplicated articles, to ensure that no conflict will be created with the amendment.

**Here's an example:**

An Association's rules allowing cumulative voting was written in the Articles of Incorporation and the CC&R's. A sufficient number of community members voted to amend the Articles, thereby removing cumulative voting. But wait! The board apparently missed the fact that the CC&R's had a duplicate section that allowed for cumulative voting. Consequently, amending the Articles of Incorporation was futile since the CC&R's take precedence; as a result, cumulative voting was still allowed.

(As of this writing, some Arizona legislators are attempting to get a bill passed that will make cumulative voting illegal, but it failed in the 2017 legislature)

# BYLAWS

When the community association is formed, usually as a non-profit corporation, the association will develop a set of Bylaws.

The Bylaws will typically include:

- Rules for member meetings,
- Quorum requirements,
- Minimum and maximum number of directors required on the board,
- Directors' term of office,
- Method of election and removal of directors,
- Meetings and types of director meetings,
- Powers of the board of directors,
- Duties of the board of directors,
- The election of officers, and their duties,
- Committees,
- Books and records, and
- Instructions for amending the Bylaws (usually an affirmative vote of 2/3 of the association members voting is needed to affect an amendment).

It's important for all directors to understand the powers of the board as set forth in the Bylaws, and equally important to know and understand the duties of the board, and the duties of each director and officer.

Typical board duties will include the following:

- Supervise all officers, agents and employees of the association and see that their duties are properly performed,

- See that a complete record of all its acts and corporate affairs are maintained. In Arizona, ARS 10-11601 lists the records a corporation is required to keep.
- Determine the annual assessments (dues),
- Have adequate insurance on the association property, and
- Cause the maintenance responsibilities to be performed.

If the board is responsible to see that all of the above is done, then it seems logical that they must set up some type of oversight procedure, such as assigning staff or a committee consisting of one or more board members to conduct periodic inspections of the association documents and property. Otherwise, how can a board know that their duties are being properly performed?

# CC&R's

The CC&R's discussion was saved for last because it is typically the most extensive of the HOA documents, and the document that takes precedence over both the Articles of Incorporation and the Bylaws. By first becoming familiar with the Articles and Bylaws, the CC&R's are easier to grasp, in my opinion. So here we go!

The Declaration of Covenants, Conditions and Restrictions (CC&R's), sometimes referred to as the "Declaration," contains descriptions of the

type of development, boundaries, land use, and common areas that are available for use by all residents, as well as the types of dwellings in the HOA such as single family homes or condominiums, and any restrictions of use.

In the event of any language conflict between the documents, the CC&R's take precedence over both the Articles of Incorporation and the Bylaws.

The restrictions on the use of each owner's property are probably the most important aspect of the CC&R's to all owners. Since all homeowners are required to abide by the restrictions and rules in the CC&R's, it is imperative to become familiar with them. And since the board of directors is required to enforce the rules and restrictions equally among all homeowners, the directors must become familiar with them.

### Amendments

The CC&R's are the most difficult document to amend. In most Arizona associations, for the first 20 years it takes a 90% affirmative vote of all homeowners to affect an amendment. After 20 years, the percentage drops to 75% or 80% of all homeowners to vote in the affirmative, which is still virtually impossible to obtain.

Unfortunately, there are many homeowners who are complacent and will not bother to study an initiative and take the time to vote. The only time many homeowners will become active is if something directly affects their pocketbook—such as notice of a dues increase.

## RULES AND REGULATIONS

The CC&R's contain some very specific rules, and some general rules. The association also has the power to develop specific Rules and Regulations that further explain and clarify the general rules in the CC&R's. The rules *cannot* add new types of rules, and *cannot* modify nor delete any of the existing rules. The rules, as they are clarified, must also comply with the laws that govern planned communities, and cannot conflict with anything in the CC&R's.

The CC&R's take precedence over the Articles of Incorporation and the Bylaws; but state and federal laws take precedence over the CC&R's and all other association governing documents. Due to the fact that amending the CC&R's is almost impossible, there will usually be some covenants in that document that have been outdated by new law. It's important to understand that, and be on the lookout for conflict between the CC&R's and current law.

Here's an example of a conflict that gives Arizona associations more power than they may have known they have. Many associations are probably under the impression that if the streets in their community are owned and maintained by the local government, that the association cannot control street parking on those streets. However, one little known law changed that for associations established prior to 2015.

According to ARS 33-1818, if an association was established prior to December 31, 2014, an association can control parking on the community roadways notwithstanding that the roadways are owned by and maintained by a local government entity. (In gated communities, the streets are owned and maintained by the community so those communities can always control street parking.) The 2017 Arizona legislature had a bill to repeal that law, but it didn't pass.

**Here's an example** of a parking rule in an HOA's CC&R's that is further clarified in the Rules:

The covenant in the CC&R's states, "No parking on the street."

The Rules can clarify that by stating, "No overnight parking on the street." That makes sense because guests, landscapers, and other vendors have no other place to park during the day. The Rule didn't change the covenant; it just explained and clarified it.

**Here's another example:**

A covenant in the CC&R's states, "No home based business allowed."

Today, society has changed; many people have home-based businesses and some employees perform work at home for their employer. Consequently, that covenant is outdated and needs some clarification in order to meet the needs of work-at-home homeowners.

A newly established HOA rule could clarify: "No home-based business is allowed that would create more than normal community traffic, nor create excess noise or otherwise create a neighborhood nuisance." The outdated rule of "no home business allowed" is clarified and brought up-to-date by that rule. The rule allows the business as long as it doesn't negatively affect the community.

The state of Arizona has a home-based business law, and the Town of Gilbert has a home-based business guideline, both of which take precedence over the HOA rules. These will be discussed further in Chapter 4 under the State and City Laws section.

### A Rule and Law conflict

Sometimes there is a seemingly unsurmountable conflict between the law and the rules. Here is an example:

- A real estate broker owns a one-person brokerage which he runs from his home office; he doesn't create any more than normal traffic in the community.
- The HOA rules state that no signs are allowed in windows. The only allowable signs are political signs during elections, house for sale signs, or the occasional garage sale sign.
- The Arizona Department of Real Estate requires the brokerage to have a sign in a window with specific language. However, the law does not specify a size or exact location.
- The workaround is to have an index-sized card with the required language placed in the bottom corner of a window that isn't visible from the street.
  - Everyone's requirement is met!

The home-based business sign law is discussed further in Chapter 4 under the State and City Laws section.

# Governing Document Precedence

Now it's time to list the governing documents in the order of precedence.

- **CC&R's**
  - In the event of a conflict between the language of the CC&R's and the Articles of Incorporation or Bylaws, the CC&R's take precedence.
- **Articles of Incorporation**
  - In the event of a conflict between the language of the Articles of Incorporation and the Bylaws, the Articles take precedence.
- **Bylaws**
  - The language of the CC&R's and the Articles of Incorporation always take precedence over the Bylaws.

# Committees

The Board of Directors makes policy decisions and hires a manager to run the day-to-day operation of the association. There are many times when the board needs to conduct research in order to gather sufficient information to make a decision. That is where committees come in.

A committee can consist of one or more members. Committee members do not need to be board members; they should be individuals with some expertise that will be valuable to the project. They are assigned by the board along with special instructions regarding the task they are assigned. The board should also establish a reasonable deadline for the project.

In Arizona, there are two types of committees:

- Standing Committees (referred to in ARS 33-1804 as Regularly Scheduled Committees), and
- Ad Hoc Committees.

ARS 33-1804 is the Open Meeting Law, sometimes referred to as the Sunshine Law, and it requires that any Regularly Scheduled Committee meetings must be held open to all members of the association, therefore, notice of the meeting date(s) must be published.

The Bylaws will state what, if any, standing committees the association must have, such as an Architectural Review Committee, Finance Committee, Maintenance Committee, etc. The board can establish any other standing committee(s) they feel necessary.

### Ad Hoc Committees

An Ad Hoc Committee is a special committee established for only one purpose and when the project is complete, the committee is automatically dissolved. The Ad Hoc Committee, therefore, is not subject to the Open Meeting Law. It can meet at any time without providing notice to anyone except the committee members. The Ad Hoc Committee will have a chairman whose responsibility is to report the committee progress to the board at monthly meetings.

When the committee project is complete, its findings are presented to the board, along with supporting documents, and an action is typically recommended for the board to take. The board can ask questions, accept the recommendation, reject the recommendation, or request the committee to provide additional information. When the project is complete, the committee is automatically dissolved.

### Standing Committees
### Architectural Review Committee (ARC)

Each Association will usually develop a set of architectural guidelines that will specify the type of material approved for houses in the community; a paint pallet displaying the approved colors of the house and trim exterior, and the type of approved landscape including ground cover, plants and trees, etc. When a new house is being built within the community, or when a homeowner plans to modify the exterior of a house or yard, plans must be submitted to the ARC for approval.

The purpose of the guidelines is to keep a theme consistent throughout the community in order to enhance property values.

The ARC is a standing committee and must provide notice to the community of its meetings, which may be scheduled every month, depending on the volume of requests for ARC review.

The ARC members usually consist of volunteer homeowners who have some degree of experience or knowledge about building and/or contracting.

There may be times when a request for approval is rejected by the ARC for some reason, or the homeowner is asked to make some revisions, whether minor or major, and then return with an amended proposal. If the owner objects, then the ARC guidelines may have a procedure for the owner to appeal. In some cases that I'm aware of, an owner can appeal to the ARC, and the decision of the ARC after that appeal is final. In that association, the Board develops the architectural guidelines, but they do not have authority to overturn an appeal decision made by the ARC.

Occasionally, a homeowner may attempt an end run around the ARC. They may contact the property manager or a friend on the board, and have them request that the board amend the rules.

The board can amend the rules; however, the act of a director or manager allowing a member to circumvent the ARC and go directly to the board, and the board agreeing to amend the rules for one individual in that manner, can cause bad relationships and a lack of trust between the ARC members, the manager, and the board. It could also have the appearance of a conflict of interest.

In my opinion, a board should deny any attempt to circumvent the ARC. Any proposed amendment to the architectural rules should be discussed with the ARC committee members to obtain their input before the board takes an action to affect an amendment. That's because the ARC members probably know much more about the ARC rules than the manager or board members. These committee members may have helped develop all or most of the rules, and may have been working on the committee for years, while the board members and manager may be relatively new.

When a board does amend a rule, the homeowner must reapply to the ARC for approval under the new rule. The original approval was given under the old rule, therefore, is not automatically granted under the amended rules until the new application is submitted and the ARC approves the application.

CHAPTER 4

# PLANNED COMMUNITY LAWS

## ARS TITLE 10 NON-PROFIT CORPORATION LAWS

The Arizona Revised Statutes Chapters 24 through 40 of Title 10 contain the laws for non-profit corporations. This book will not discuss all of the sections in those laws; however, we will discuss a couple of the laws that

I feel are especially important for directors to understand. Similar laws governing non-profit corporations likely exist in your state. If your state doesn't have a Planned Communities Act, then talk to your association attorney to find out which of the non-profit laws are applicable to HOAs.

### *Standards of Conduct*
There will be another discussion of this section in the chapter dealing with the Business Judgment Rule. Because this law is of such importance, the entire section of the law is reproduced here with my layperson

interpretation which is also the interpretation of two attorneys with whom I discussed this law.

## Fiduciary Duties

The law below spells out what is known as the Fiduciary Duties for directors. Every director should become very familiar with these standards.

## ARS 10-3830 — General standards for directors

A. A director's duties, including duties as a member of a committee, shall be discharged:
   1. In good faith.
   2. With the care an ordinarily prudent person in a like position would exercise under similar circumstances.
   3. In a manner the director reasonably believes to be in the best interests of the corporation.

B. In discharging duties, a director is entitled to rely on information, opinions, reports or statements, including financial statements and other financial data, if prepared or presented by any of the following:
   1. One or more officers or employees of the corporation whom the director reasonably believes are reliable and competent in the matters presented.
   2. Legal counsel, public accountants or other persons as to matters the director reasonably believes are within the person's professional or expert competence.
   3. A committee of or appointed by the board of directors of which the director is not a member if the director reasonably believes the committee merits confidence.
   4. (Not applicable to non-profit HOA corporations)

C. A director is not acting in good faith if the director has knowledge concerning the matter in question that makes reliance otherwise permitted by subsection B unwarranted.

D.  A director is not liable for any action taken as a director or any failure to take any action if the director's duties were performed in compliance with this section.

In any proceeding commenced under this section or any other provision of this chapter, a director has all of the defenses and presumptions ordinarily available to a director.

A director is presumed in all cases to have acted, failed to act or otherwise discharged such director's duties in accordance with subsection A.

The burden is on the party challenging a director's action, failure to act or other discharge of duties to establish by clear and convincing evidence facts rebutting the presumption.

E.  (This subsection is not applicable to HOA corporations.)

## *My Comments*

This law is powerful for a board or individual director accused of wrongdoing by an unhappy homeowner, or for a director accused by a board of wrongdoing.

Subsection A consists of the fiduciary duties owed to the association by the board and by individual directors, and is what courts refer to when applying the Business Judgment Rule.

Subsection B provides that a director, or the board, is entitled to rely on information from professional counsel — provided (in subsection C), that there is no reason to believe that reliance on that counsel is unwarranted.

Subsection C is especially important to understand. Once a director or board has information indicating that the information provided by an advisor is unwarranted, the director, or the board, is no longer warranted in following that advice.

If the director meets the criteria in subsections A and B, the director is presumed to have acted properly.

The following statement is crucial to remember: The burden of proof is on the accuser to prove by **clear and convincing evidence** that the director or board did not act in accordance with this section.

## Definitions

The United States Ninth Circuit Court defines clear and convincing evidence in subsection 1.7 of their Trial Process Instructions:

When a party has the burden of proving any claim or defense by clear and convincing evidence, it means that the party must present evidence that leaves you with a firm belief or conviction that it is highly probable that the factual contentions of the claim or defense are true. This is a higher standard of proof than proof by a preponderance of the evidence, but it does not require proof beyond a reasonable doubt.

## ARS 10-3851 — Authority to indemnify

This law should be comforting to directors and boards because it provides that the association may indemnify a director against liability if the director was complying with his or her fiduciary duties as spelled out in ARS 10-3830, subsection A, above.

## ARS 10-3852 — Mandatory indemnification

A. Unless limited by its Articles of Incorporation, a corporation **shall** indemnify a director who was the prevailing party, on the merits or otherwise, in the defense of any proceeding to which the director was a party because the director is or was a director of the corporation against reasonable expenses incurred by the director in connection with the proceeding. As long as the conditions are met, this law requires mandatory indemnification.

## My Comments

Some associations have an indemnification section in their Bylaws.

If a complainant believes that one or more board members are violating their fiduciary duties, that complainant, in addition to suing the association, can also sue each board member individually. Therefore, it should be a requirement that, in addition to any state laws on indemnification, the association Bylaws should have a mandatory indemnity section, and the association should carry Directors and Officers (D&O) insurance for all directors and committee members.

# ARS 33 Planned Community Laws

In this section we'll discuss four planned community laws from Title 33. The laws are numbered from 33-1801 through 33-1818. We'll discuss 1804, 1805, 1811, and 1813 first, and make some comments. Then the remaining sections will be printed in full in numerical order without any discussion. They are printed in the book for your convenience to read and become familiar with. Remember that laws may change each year. In Arizona, the legislative session ends in May and the new laws become effective in August. The laws in this book reflect the changes made in 2017.

### 33-1804. Open meetings; exceptions
Notwithstanding any provision in the declaration, bylaws or other documents to the contrary, all meetings of the members' association and the board of directors, and any regularly scheduled committee meetings, are open to all members of the association or any person designated by a member in writing as the member's representative and all members or designated representatives so desiring shall be permitted to attend and speak at an appropriate time during the deliberations and proceedings.

The board of directors, any committees of the board of directors and the membership may take action only if there is a quorum present for the board, committee or membership meeting and the meeting is held as prescribed in this section.

The board may place reasonable time restrictions on those persons speaking during the meeting but shall permit a member or member's designated representative to speak once after the board has discussed a specific agenda item but before the board takes formal action on that item in addition to any other opportunities to speak. The board shall provide for a reasonable number of persons to speak on each side of an issue.

Persons attending may audiotape or videotape those portions of the meetings of the board of directors and meetings of the members that are open. The board of directors of the association may adopt reasonable rules governing the audiotaping and videotaping of open portions of the meetings of the board and the membership, but such rules shall not preclude such audiotaping or videotaping by those attending and shall not require advance notice of the audiotaping or videotaping. Any portion of a meeting may be closed only if that closed portion of the meeting is limited to consideration of one or more of the following:

1.  Legal advice from an attorney for the board or the association. On final resolution of any matter for which the board received legal advice or that concerned pending or contemplated litigation, the board may disclose information about that matter in an open meeting except for matters that are required to remain confidential by the terms of a settlement agreement or judgment.

2.  Pending or contemplated litigation.

3.  Personal, health or financial information about an individual member of the association, an individual employee of the association or an individual employee of a contractor for the association, including records of the association directly related to the personal, health or financial information about an individual member of the association, an individual employee of the association or an individual employee of a contractor for the association.

4.  Matters relating to the job performance of, compensation of, health records of or specific complaints against an individual employee of the association or an individual employee of a contractor of the association who works under the direction of the association.

5.  Discussion of a member's appeal of any violation cited or penalty imposed by the association except on request of the affected member that the meeting be held in an open session.

6.  At the discretion of the board of directors, violations of the declaration or assessment delinquencies. If violations of the declaration or assessment delinquencies are considered in a closed meeting, the

board of directors shall report during an open portion of that meeting immediately following the closed meeting the number of violation notices sent and the number and dollar amounts of any delinquent assessments occurring since the last meeting of the board of directors.

B.  Notwithstanding any provision in the community documents, all meetings of the members' association and the board shall be held in this state. A meeting of the members' association shall be held at least once each year. Special meetings of the members' association may be called by the president, by a majority of the board of directors or by members having at least twentyfive percent, or any lower percentage specified in the bylaws, of the votes in the association. Not fewer than ten nor more than fifty days in advance of any meeting of the members the secretary shall cause notice to be handdelivered or sent prepaid by United States mail to the mailing address for each lot, parcel or unit owner or to any other mailing address designated in writing by a member. The notice shall state the date, time and place of the meeting. A notice of any annual, regular or special meeting of the members shall also state the purpose for which the meeting is called, including the general nature of any proposed amendment to the declaration or bylaws, changes in assessments that require approval of the members and any proposal to remove a director or an officer. The failure of any member to receive actual notice of a meeting of the members does not affect the validity of any action taken at that meeting.

C.  For any closed portion of a meeting of the board of directors as pre-scribed by subsection A of this section, the board shall make available an agenda that includes a description of the specific exemption that provides the basis for the portion of the meeting to be closed and shall make available that agenda to the members before the closed portion of the meeting is held. The agenda for the closed portion of a meeting, including the specific exemption, shall be attached to the minutes of the open portion of the meeting.

D. Notwithstanding any provision in the declaration, bylaws or other community documents, for meetings of the board of directors that are held after the termination of declarant control of the association, notice to members of meetings of the board of directors shall be given at least fortyeight hours in advance of the meeting by newsletter, conspicuous posting or any other reasonable means as determined by the board of directors. An affidavit of notice by an officer of the corporation is prima facie evidence that notice was given as prescribed by this section. Notice to members of meetings of the board of directors is not required if emergency circumstances require action by the board before notice can be given. Any notice of a board meeting shall state the date, time and place of the meeting. The failure of any member to receive actual notice of a meeting of the board of directors does not affect the validity of any action taken at that meeting.

E. Notwithstanding any provision in the declaration, bylaws or other community documents, for meetings of the board of directors or committees of the board of directors that are held after the termination of declarant control of the association, all of the following apply:
   1. Notice of the meeting must be provided at least forty-eight hours before the meeting.
   2. The agenda shall be available to all members attending.
   3. An emergency meeting of the board of directors may be called to discuss business or take action that cannot be delayed for the fortyeight hours required for notice. At any emergency meeting called by the board of directors, the board of directors may act only on emergency matters at that emergency meeting and may not take action on nonemergency matters.

   An emergency meeting may be conducted by way of a telephone conference call, internetbased livemeeting system or other form of technology instead of by way of a personal meeting. An emergency meeting may be conducted without member presence or participation. The minutes of the emergency meeting shall state the reason necessitating the emergency meeting. The minutes of the emergency meeting shall be read and approved at the next regularly scheduled meeting of the board of directors.

4.  A quorum of the board of directors may meet by means of a telephone conference if a speakerphone is available in the meeting room that allows board members and association members to hear all parties who are speaking during the meeting.

5.  Any quorum of the board of directors that meets informally to discuss association business, including workshops, shall comply with the open meeting and notice provisions of this section without regard to whether the board votes or takes any action on any matter at that informal meeting.

F.  It is the policy of this state as reflected in this section that all meetings of a planned community, whether meetings of the members' association or meetings of the board of directors of the association, be conducted openly and that notices and agendas be provided for those meetings that contain the information that is reasonably necessary to inform the members of the matters to be discussed or decided and to ensure that members have the ability to speak after discussion of agenda items, but before a vote of the board of directors or members is taken. Toward this end, any person or entity that is charged with the interpretation of these provisions, including members of the board of directors and ANY community manager, shall take into account this declaration of policy and shall construe any provision of this section in favor of open meetings.

## My Comments

The open meeting law is sometimes referred to as the Sunshine Law; this law requires that all meetings of the board of directors be open to members of the association, except those described in Subsection A, 1 through 5, that may be held in closed executive session.

Members shall have a reasonable opportunity to speak on an issue after the board has discussed it and prior to the board voting.

A reasonable time limit may be imposed for each speaker, and the number of speakers may be limited.

It is advisable to alternate between speakers who are opposed and who favor the issue.

Members may take video of the meeting, and the association may develop reasonable rules for videotaping.

The board **may** meet in closed (sometimes referred to as executive) session for the following reasons:

1. Legal advice from an attorney.
2. Pending or contemplated litigation.
3. Personal, health or financial information about an individual member of the association, or of employees.
4. Job performance of, compensation, health records, or specific complaints against an individual employee of the association.
5. Discussion of a member's appeal of any violation cited or penalty imposed by the association, except on request of the affected member that the meeting be held in an open session. (This gives the member the option of having their hearing held in open session.)

The word **"may"** is emphasized above because the law gives the board the discretion. However, Arizona HOA attorney Jonathan Olcott and others with whom I've spoken say it is a best practice to treat the word "may" as "shall" because it's possible for some federal laws to be violated if the board discusses certain personal information in an open meeting.

### 33-1805. Association financial and other records

A. Except as provided in subsection B of this section, all financial and other records of the association shall be made reasonably available for examination by any member or any person designated by the member in writing as the member's representative. The association shall not charge a member or any person designated by the member in writing for making material available for review. The association shall have ten business days to fulfill a request for examination. On request for purchase of copies of records by any member or any person designated by the member in writing as the member's representative, the association shall have ten business days to provide copies of the requested records. An association may charge a fee for making copies of not more than fifteen cents per page.

B. Books and records kept by or on behalf of the association and the board may be withheld from disclosure to the extent that the portion withheld relates to any of the following:
   1. Privileged communication between an attorney for the association and the association.
   2. Pending litigation.
   3. Meeting minutes or other records of a session of a board meeting that is not required to be open to all members pursuant to section 33-1804.
   4. Personal, health or financial records of an individual member of the association, an individual employee of the association or an individual employee of a contractor for the association, including records of the association directly related to the personal, health or financial information about an individual member of the association, an individual employee of the association or an individual employee of a contractor for the association.
   5. Records relating to the job performance of, compensation of, health records of or specific complaints against an individual employee of the association or an individual employee of a contractor of the association who works under the direction of the association.

C. The association shall not be required to disclose financial and other records of the association if disclosure would violate any state or federal law.

### My Comments
Two attorneys that I'm aware of have stated that an association may require, as a condition of a member obtaining records, that the member

 fill out a questionnaire stating that the member avows to not use the records for certain purposes.

Three other attorneys I have spoken with about this matter said that the law does not allow an association to require a questionnaire.

The language below appears to me to agree with the three latter attorneys who say the law does not allow the association to request a questionnaire.

ARS 33-1805 states:

> *"...all financial and other records of the association shall be made **reasonably available** for examination by any member..."*

My question is how a court will interpret the words *"reasonably available?"*

- Does the law, as written, allow an association to tell a homeowner what she can and cannot do with the requested records?
- Is it reasonable to require a homeowner to fill out a questionnaire and avow that she won't do something with the information?

Ultimately, if the questionnaire is challenged in court, the judge will determine that answer. This is food for thought in the event that your association elects to require a questionnaire to be filled out prior to providing requested documents to a homeowner.

Before we leave this subject, let's take a look at the non-profit corporation law, Title 10 Section 11602. If there is no conflicting law in the planned community laws of Title 33, then Title 10 controls.

Below is the entire Section 11602. After you read this, then we'll again attempt to answer the question "Is it reasonable to require a homeowner to fill out a questionnaire and avow that she won't do something with the information."

Pay particular attention to Subsections C and G.

## ARS 10-11602

A.  Subject to subsections E and F of this section, any member who has been a member of record at least six months immediately preceding its demand is entitled to inspect and copy any of the records of the corporation described in section 10-11601, subsection E during regular business hours at the corporation's principal office, if the member gives the corporation written notice of its demand as provided in section 10-3141 at least five business days before the date on which the member wishes to inspect and copy.

B.  Subject to subsections E and F of this section, a member who has been a member of record at least six months immediately preceding its demand is entitled to inspect and copy any of the following records of the corporation during regular business hours at a reasonable location specified by the corporation, if the member meets the requirements of subsection C of this section and gives the corporation written notice of its demand as provided in section 10-3141 at least five business days before the date on which the member wishes to inspect and copy the following:

1.  Excerpts from any records required to be maintained under section 10-11601, subsection A, to the extent not subject to inspection under subsection A of this section.
2.  Accounting records of the corporation.
3.  Subject to section 10-11605, the membership list described in section 10-11601, subsection C.
4.  The corporation's most recent financial statements showing in reasonable detail its assets and liabilities and the results of its operations.

C. A member may inspect and copy the records identified in subsection B of this section only if the following conditions are met:
1. The member's demand is made in good faith and for a proper purpose.
2. The member describes with reasonable particularity the member's purpose and the records the member desires to inspect.
3. The records are directly connected with the member's purpose.

D. This section does not affect either:
1. The right of a member to inspect records under section 10-3720 or, if the member is in litigation with the corporation, to the same extent as any other litigant.
2. The power of a court, independently of chapters 24 through 40 of this title, to compel the production of corporate records for examination on proof by a member of proper purpose.

E. The articles of incorporation or bylaws of a corporation organized primarily for religious purposes may limit or abolish the right of a member under this section to inspect and copy any corporate record.

F. Unless the board of directors has provided express permission to the member, a member of a corporation that is a rural electric cooperative is not entitled to inspect or copy any records, documents or other materials that are maintained by or in the possession of the corporation and that relate to any of the following:
1. Personnel matters or a person's medical records.
2. Communications between an attorney for the corporation and the corporation.
3. Pending or contemplated litigation.
4. Pending or contemplated matters relating to enforcement of the corporation's documents or rules.

G. This section does not apply to any corporation that is a condominium as defined in section 33-1202 or a planned community as defined in section 33-1802.

H. This section does not apply to timeshare plans or associations that are subject to title 33, chapter 20.

## My Comments

Subsection C of 11602 places restrictions on what the person requesting records can do with them. It requires that the records be for a particular purpose and that the person must state the reason for the records request.

Subsection G states that this section, 11602, does not apply to planned communities as defined in ARS 33-1802. Therefore, it is my layman opinion that a corporation who is a planned community must comply with ARS 33-1805, and must make the records "reasonably" available to the member; they cannot require a member to state a purpose, and fill out a questionnaire, as is allowed under Title 10-11602.

## ARS 33-1811. Board of directors; contracts; conflict

If any contract, decision or other action for compensation taken by or on behalf of the board of directors would benefit any member of the board of directors or any person who is a parent, grandparent, spouse, child or sibling of a member of the board of directors or a parent or spouse of any of those persons, that member of the board of directors shall declare a conflict of interest for that issue. The member shall declare the conflict in an open meeting of the board before the board discusses or takes action on that issue and that member may then vote on that issue. Any contract entered into in violation of this section is void and unenforceable.

## ARS 10-3860

In this article, unless the context otherwise requires:

1. "Conflicting interest" with respect to a corporation means the interest a director of the corporation has respecting a transaction effected

or proposed to be effected by the corporation, by a subsidiary of the corporation or by any other entity in which the corporation has a controlling interest if either:

a. Whether or not the transaction is brought before the board of directors of the corporation for action, the director knows at the time of commitment that the director or a related person either:

    i. Is a party to the transaction.

    ii. Has a beneficial financial interest in or is so closely linked to the transaction and of such financial significance to the director or a related person that the interest would reasonably be expected to exert an influence on the director's judgment if he were called on to vote on the transaction.

b. The transaction is brought or is of such character and significance to the corporation that it would in the normal course be brought before the board of directors of the corporation for action, and the director knows at the time of commitment that any of the following persons is either a party to the transaction or has a beneficial financial interest in or is so closely linked to the transaction and of such financial significance to the person that the interest would reasonably be expected to exert an influence on the director's judgment if the director were called on to vote on the transaction....

## My Comments

**Attorney Jonathan Olcott, of Philip Brown and Jonathan Olcott (PB&J) in Phoenix,** provided the following statements regarding conflicts of interest:

> *"Another way to look at conflict of interest is loyalty. Directors owe a fiduciary duty of undivided loyalty to the corporation..."*

Mr. Olcott went on to say:

*"We hear the term "conflict of interest" often, but what does it mean? A conflict of interest exists when you have divided loyalty. Arizona law provides that a director owes a fiduciary duty of undivided loyalty to the corporation."*

Consider this scenario:

*"A director's friend owns a landscape company. The Association goes out to bid for a landscaper, and the friend submits a bid. The director may think that because she gets no money from the transaction, she does not have a conflict of interest. On the other hand, the director has feelings of loyalty to her friend. Her loyalty to the corporation is not undivided. Her loyalty is divided between the corporation and her friend. Based on this, she realizes she has a conflict of interest. She is now obligated to take the legal steps required when a director has a conflict of interest."*

The subject of director conflict of interest is covered in both the non-profit statute ARS 10-3860 and the planned community statute, ARS 33-1811 printed above. The association Bylaws may also have a section on conflicts of interest.

ARS 33-1811 states that if a contract or decision would benefit any member of a board of directors, that must be disclosed prior to a discussion on the issue taking place, and after disclosure that member may vote on the issue.

ARS 10-3860 doesn't state it, but implies, in (b) above, that the director should not vote on the issue.

Title 33 is for planned communities, therefore, it is my layperson opinion that ARS 33-1811 would apply, and the director, after disclosure, would be allowed to vote on the issue. The director should consider how the other directors and community members will perceive the potential of a conflict.

Would the director being in the room during the debate and subsequent vote have the appearance of making the other directors uncomfortable in their discussion? Would the director's attendance in the room have any influence on other directors' debate and vote? Those are questions the director should answer for herself, and then make whatever decision she feels is best for the association.

## ARS 33-1813. *Removal of board member; special meeting*

A.  Notwithstanding any provision of the declaration or bylaws to the contrary, the members, by a majority vote of members entitled to vote and voting on the matter at a meeting of the members called pursuant to this section at which a quorum is present, may remove any member of the board of directors with or without cause, other than a member appointed by the declarant. For purposes of calling for removal of a member of the board of directors, other than a member appointed by the declarant, the following apply:

1.  In an association with one thousand or fewer members, on receipt of a petition that calls for removal of a member of the board of directors and that is signed by the number of persons who are entitled to cast at least twenty-five per cent of the votes in the association or one hundred votes in the association, whichever is less, the board shall call and provide written notice of a special meeting of the association as prescribed by section 33-1804, subsection B.

2.  Notwithstanding section 33-1804, subsection B, in an association with more than one thousand members, on receipt of a petition that calls for removal of a member of the board of directors and that is signed by the number of persons who are entitled to cast at least ten per cent of the votes in the association or one thousand votes in the association, whichever is less, the board shall call and provide written notice of a special meeting of the association. The board shall provide written notice of a special meeting as prescribed by section 33-1804, subsection B.

3.  The special meeting shall be called, noticed and held within thirty days after receipt of the petition.

4.  For purposes of a special meeting called pursuant to this subsection, a quorum is present if the number of owners to whom at least

twenty per cent of the votes or one thousand votes, whichever is less, are allocated is present at the meeting in person or as otherwise permitted by law.

5.  If a civil action is filed regarding the removal of a board member, the prevailing party in the civil action shall be awarded its reasonable attorney fees and costs.

6.  The board of directors shall retain all documents and other records relating to the proposed removal of the member of the board of directors for at least one year after the date of the special meeting and shall permit members to inspect those documents and records pursuant to section 33-1805.

7.  A petition that calls for the removal of the same member of the board of directors shall not be submitted more than once during each term of office for that member.

B.  For an association in which board members are elected from separately designated voting districts, a member of the board of directors, other than a member appointed by the declarant, may be removed only by a vote of the members from that voting district, and only the members from that voting district are eligible to vote on the matter or be counted for purposes of determining a quorum.

## *My Comments*

The non-profit corporation laws have a section, ARS 10-3808, that also deals with the removal of a director by members of the association, and the procedure is quite different than ARS 33-1813. In this case, since there is a procedure in 33-1813 specifically outlined for HOA's, 33-1813 takes precedence.

Removal of one or more directors is rather straight forward, but it is wise for the association to have the entire process overseen by the association attorney to be certain that the appropriate procedures and laws are followed.

## Transfer of Home Ownership

Many directors are not familiar with ARS 33-1806 that governs the resale of homes because the subject of homeownership transfer is rarely discussed in board meetings. However, I believe it is important for all directors to be familiar with this law because if it isn't complied with the association could be at legal financial risk.

The property manager is assigned the duty of providing the disclosure package to the title company within ten days after receiving the request, and because it is a management duty, the directors never see those requests. Nevertheless, the board has the responsibility of knowing that the information in the package meets the statutory requirements, and that it is provided within the mandatory time frame.

In Chapter 5, Directors and Officers Duties, you'll learn that one duty of the board of directors is to

> "Supervise all officers, agents and employees of the Association, and to see that their duties are properly performed".

Section B. of ARS 33-1806 states:

> "A purchaser or seller who is damaged by the failure of the member or the association to disclose the information required by subsection A of this section may pursue all remedies at law or in equity against the member or the association, whichever failed to comply with subsection A of this section, including the recovery of reasonable attorney fees."

Consequently, if a buyer is damaged by not receiving all of the required information, the board is responsible. This can be prevented if the board of directors do their job of supervising the agents and employees and see that their duties are properly performed. It means that the board should conduct periodic inspections. An Oversight Committee, such as that described in Chapter 5, is one method of conducting the inspections.

What follows is a full discussion and reprint of the statute, ARS 33-1806, which should be beneficial to board members, homebuyers and Realtors.

A seller, or if the community has 50 or more units, the HOA management company, is required to provide specific disclosure documents to buyers in accordance with ARS 33-1806.

When a home purchase contract is placed in escrow, the escrow officer is required to "promptly" notify the seller or the HOA management of the pending sale, and request the disclosure documents. The seller, or the HOA, has ten days after receiving the request to deliver those documents to the escrow officer, who in turn passes the documents on to the buyer. However, some not-so-conscientious escrow agents may not give the documents to the buyer until they come in to sign the sale and finance documents just several days prior to the close of escrow — and the buyer may not read the documents.

Nevertheless, the law presumes that the buyer has read and understood the documents, and in fact, the buyer must sign a statement that they have read the documents and understand they are entering into a contract with the HOA.

Homebuyers who have never lived in an HOA community may not be aware of these requirements, and even many who have previously lived in one, may not be aware. If the title company delays sending the disclosure request, and the HOA takes the full ten days to provide HOA documents, that may leave little time for a buyer to study the documents during a typical thirty (30) day escrow.

Therefore, in certain cases, where the buyer has specific community requirements, it may be worthwhile for the buyers to ask the escrow officer to immediately request the documents, and pay the "up to" one hundred dollar rush fee for the HOA to produce the documents within 72 hours so there is plenty of time to study them.

Just imagine that you plan to park a boat or an RV on your lot and the CC&R's say that is prohibited; you will be very disappointed if you haven't read the CC&R's because your boat or RV will have to find another storage space.

If you want a desert front yard landscape, and the rules require grass, then you cannot have your desert landscape.

Every homebuyer should do their due diligence and understand what type of community they're buying into, and learn the rules that govern that community so they will not be disappointed after moving in. Realtors should do their part in educating their clients about what to expect when buying into an HOA community.

Buyers should pay special attention to ARS 33-1806 A.3. (e) below, whereby if there is an "apparent" violation on the property that is not on the association's records at the time ownership is transferred, the "buyer" is responsible!

**That's worth repeating!**

If there is an "apparent" violation on the property that is not on the association's records at the time the property ownership is transferred—that is, the close of escrow date—the "buyer" is responsible! That's right, it is the law. An HOA can, and probably will, hold the buyer to that law.

That's a tough one, and shouldn't be that way because unless buyers know what to look for, they will not be able to determine if there is an "apparent" violation on the property. One possible way to prevent getting stuck with a potentially costly violation, could be to have the buyer request the manager to perform a current inspection of the property and/or provide written assurance that there are no "apparent" violations.

It could get fairly expensive if the seller painted the house a non-approved color and the association hadn't yet noticed, and refuses to provide an exception for the color. That isn't as far-fetched as it may seem.

## Disclosure Fee

The documents the association is required by ARS 33-1806 to furnish buyers are called "disclosure documents." The association can charge a fee of up to $400 for that service. Many times it is broken down into a Transfer

Fee and a Disclosure Fee, with part of that fee going to the management company and the other part going to the association. The buyer and seller can negotiate who pays that fee. They can agree to split the fee 50/50, or in some cases, either the buyer or seller can agree to pay the full fee. No matter how the association names the fees, the total aggregate amount they can charge for the disclosure document service is $400.

### Capital Improvement Fee

There is one more little caveat. Well, maybe not so little…

An association can charge more than the $400 fee—but you won't find that information in the law.

The maximum $400 fee is for the service of providing the legally required documents to the buyer. ARS 33-1806 does not authorize, but neither does it preclude, an association from charging a "capital improvement fee," a "reserve fund fee," or another type of fee where the money is going into a special purpose fund that benefits the community. Therefore, if either the CC&R's or the Bylaws give the association the power to charge a special one-time fee for "capital improvements," etc., and that purpose is spelled out in the governing documents, the association can charge that fee.

This fee can be in the thousands of dollars.

The good news is that I've never seen that type of fee charged by the average HOA in Phoenix. As I mentioned, it can only be charged if it is specifically authorized in the governing documents. If it isn't found in the governing documents, and the board asks the homeowners to vote to approve the fee, homeowners would likely vote it down because it may make it more difficult to sell homes in the community. A reduction in the number of sales could then result in lower property values.

Here is the complete Arizona law:

### ARS 33-1806

A. For planned communities with fewer than fifty units, a member shall mail or deliver to a purchaser or a purchaser's authorized agent within ten days after receipt of a written notice of a pending sale of the unit, and for planned communities with fifty or more units, the association shall mail or deliver to a purchaser or a purchaser's authorized agent within ten days after receipt of a written notice of a pending sale that contains the name and address of the purchaser all of the following in either paper or electronic format:

1. A copy of the bylaws and the rules of the association.
2. A copy of the declaration.
3. A dated statement containing:
   a. The telephone number and address of a principal contact for the association, which may be an association manager, an association management company, an officer of the association or any other person designated by the board of directors.
   b. The amount of the common regular assessment and the unpaid common regular assessment, special assessment or other assessment, fee or charge currently due and payable from the selling member. If the request is made by a lien holder, escrow agent, member or person designated by a member pursuant to section 33-1807, failure to provide the information pursuant to this subdivision within the time provided for in this subsection shall extinguish any lien for any unpaid assessment then due against that property.
   c. A statement as to whether a portion of the unit is covered by insurance maintained by the association.
   d. The total amount of money held by the association as reserves.
   e. If the statement is being furnished by the association, a statement as to whether the records of the association reflect any alterations or improvements to the unit that violate the declaration. The association is not obligated to provide information regarding alterations or improvements that occurred more than six years before the proposed sale. Nothing in this subdivision relieves the seller of a unit from the obligation to disclose alterations or improvements to the unit that violate the declaration, **nor precludes the association from taking action against the purchaser of a unit for violations that are**

**apparent at the time of purchase and that are not reflected in the association's records.**

f. If the statement is being furnished by the member, a statement as to whether the member has any knowledge of any alterations or improvements to the unit that violate the declaration.

g. A statement of case names and case numbers for pending litigation with respect to the unit filed by the association against the member or filed by the member against the association. The member shall not be required to disclose information concerning such pending litigation that would violate any applicable rule of attorney-client privilege under Arizona law.

h. A statement that provides "I hereby acknowledge that the declaration, bylaws and rules of the association constitute a contract between the association and me (the purchaser). **By signing this statement, I acknowledge that I have read and understand the association's contract with me (the purchaser).** I also understand that as a matter of Arizona law, if I fail to pay my association assessments, the association may foreclose on my property." The statement shall also include a signature line for the purchaser and shall be returned to the association within fourteen calendar days.

4. A copy of the current operating budget of the association.

5. A copy of the most recent annual financial report of the association. If the report is more than ten pages, the association may provide a summary of the report in lieu of the entire report.

6. A copy of the most recent reserve study of the association, if any.

7. A statement summarizing any pending lawsuits, except those relating to the collection of assessments owed by members other than the selling member, in which the association is a named party, including the amount of any money claimed.

B. A purchaser or seller who is damaged by the failure of the member or the association to disclose the information required by subsection A of this section may pursue all remedies at law or in equity against the member or the association, whichever failed to comply with subsection A of this section, including the recovery of reasonable attorney fees.

C. The association may charge the member a fee of no more than an aggregate of four hundred dollars to compensate the association for the costs incurred in the preparation of a statement or other documents furnished by the association pursuant to this section for purposes of resale disclosure, lien estoppel and any other services related to the transfer or use of the property. In addition, the association may charge a rush fee of no more than one hundred dollars if the rush services are required to be performed within seventy-two hours after the request for rush services, and may charge a statement or other documents update fee of no more than fifty dollars if thirty days or more have passed since the date of the original disclosure statement or the date the documents were delivered.

The association shall make available to any interested party the amount of any fee established from time to time by the association. If the aggregate fee for purposes of resale disclosure, lien estoppel and any other services related to the transfer or use of a property is less than four hundred dollars on January 1, 2010, the fee may increase at a rate of no more than twenty per cent per year based on the immediately preceding fiscal year's amount not to exceed the four hundred dollar aggregate fee.

The association may charge the same fee without regard to whether the association is furnishing the statement or other documents in paper or electronic format.

D. The fees prescribed by this section shall be collected no earlier than at the close of escrow and may only be charged once to a member for that transaction between the parties specified in the notice required pursuant to subsection A of this section. An association shall not charge or collect a fee relating to services for resale disclosure, lien estoppel and any other services related to the transfer or use of a property except as specifically authorized in this section. An association that charges or collects a fee in violation of this section is subject to a civil penalty of no more than one thousand two hundred dollars.

### List of ARS Title 33 laws that haven't been discussed
Below are the rest of the planned community laws from 1801 through 1818 in numerical order, with the exception of 1804, 1805, 1811, and 1813 that have already been discussed.

### ARS 33-1801. Applicability; exemption
A.  This chapter applies to all planned communities.

B.  Notwithstanding any provisions in the community documents, this chapter does not apply to any school that receives monies from this state, including a charter school, and a school is exempt from regulation or any enforcement action by any homeowners' association that is subject to this chapter. With the exception of homeschools as defined in section 15-802, schools shall not be established within the living units of a homeowners' association. The homeowners' association may enter into a contractual agreement with a school district or charter school to allow use of the homeowners' association's common areas by the school district or charter school.

C.  This chapter does not apply to timeshare plans or associations that are subject to chapter 20 of this title.

### ARS 33-1802. Definitions
In this chapter and in the community documents, unless the context otherwise requires:

1.  "Association" means a nonprofit corporation or unincorporated association of owners that is created pursuant to a declaration to own and operate portions of a planned community and that has the power under the declaration to assess association members to pay the costs and

expenses incurred in the performance of the association's obligations under the declaration.

2. "Community documents" means the declaration, bylaws, articles of incorporation, if any, and rules, if any.

3. "Declaration" means any instruments, however denominated, that establish a planned community and any amendment to those instruments.

4. "Planned community" means a real estate development that includes real estate owned and operated by or real estate on which an easement to maintain roadways or a covenant to maintain roadways is held by a nonprofit corporation or unincorporated association of owners, that is created for the purpose of managing, maintaining or improving the property and in which the owners of separately owned lots, parcels or units are mandatory members and are required to pay assessments to the association for these purposes. Planned community does not include a timeshare plan or a timeshare association that is governed by chapter 20 of this title or a condominium that is governed by chapter 9 of this title.

## ARS 33-1803. Assessment limitation; penalties; notice to member of violation

A. Unless limitations in the community documents would result in a lower limit for the assessment, the association shall not impose a regular assessment that is more than twenty percent greater than the immediately preceding fiscal year's assessment without the approval of the majority of the members of the association. Unless reserved to the members of the association, the board of directors may impose reasonable charges for the late payment of assessments. A payment by a member is deemed late if it is unpaid fifteen or more days after its due date, unless the community documents provide for a longer period. Charges for the late payment of assessments are limited to the greater of fifteen dollars or ten percent of the amount of the unpaid assessment and may be imposed only after the association has provided notice that the assessment is overdue or provided notice that the assessment is considered overdue after a certain date. Any monies paid by the member for an unpaid assessment shall be applied first to the principal amount unpaid and then to the interest accrued.

B.  After notice and an opportunity to be heard, the board of directors may impose reasonable monetary penalties on members for violations of the declaration, bylaws and rules of the association. Notwithstanding any provision in the community documents, the board of directors shall not impose a charge for a late payment of a penalty that exceeds the greater of fifteen dollars or ten percent of the amount of the unpaid penalty. A payment is deemed late if it is unpaid fifteen or more days after its due date, unless the declaration, bylaws or rules of the association provide for a longer period. Any monies paid by a member for an unpaid penalty shall be applied first to the principal amount unpaid and then to the interest accrued. Notice pursuant to this subsection shall include information pertaining to the manner in which the penalty shall be enforced.

C.  A member who receives a written notice that the condition of the property owned by the member is in violation of the community documents without regard to whether a monetary penalty is imposed by the notice may provide the association with a written response by sending the response by certified mail within twenty-one calendar days after the date of the notice. The response shall be sent to the address identified in the notice.

D.  Within ten business days after receipt of the certified mail containing the response from the member, the association shall respond to the member with a written explanation regarding the notice that shall provide at least the following information unless previously provided in the notice of violation:

1. The provision of the community documents that has allegedly been violated.
2. The date of the violation or the date the violation was observed.
3. The first and last name of the person or persons who observed the violation.
4. The process the member must follow to contest the notice.

E. Unless the information required in subsection D, paragraph 4 of this section is provided in the notice of violation, the association shall not proceed with any action to enforce the community documents, including the collection of attorney fees, before or during the time prescribed by subsection D of this section regarding the exchange of information between the association and the member and shall give the member written notice of the member's option to petition for an administrative hearing on the matter in the state Real Estate Department pursuant to section 32-2199.01. At any time before or after completion of the exchange of information pursuant to this section, the member may petition for a hearing pursuant to section 32-2199.01 if the dispute is within the jurisdiction of the state real estate department as prescribed in section 32-2199.01.

## ARS 33-1806. Resale of units; information required; fees; civil penalty; definition

A. For planned communities with fewer than fifty units, a member shall mail or deliver to a purchaser or a purchaser's authorized agent within ten days after receipt of a written notice of a pending sale of the unit, and for planned communities with fifty or more units, the association shall mail or deliver to a purchaser or a purchaser's authorized agent within ten days after receipt of a written notice of a pending sale that contains the name and address of the purchaser all of the following in either paper or electronic format:
1. A copy of the bylaws and the rules of the association.
2. A copy of the declaration.
3. A dated statement containing:

a.	The telephone number and address of a principal contact for the association, which may be an association manager, an association management company, an officer of the association or any other person designated by the board of directors.

b.	The amount of the common regular assessment and the unpaid common regular assessment, special assessment or other assessment, fee or charge currently due and payable from the selling member. If the request is made by a lienholder, escrow agent, member or person designated by a member pursuant to section 33-1807, failure to provide the information pursuant to this subdivision within the time provided for in this subsection shall extinguish any lien for any unpaid assessment then due against that property.

c.	A statement as to whether a portion of the unit is covered by insurance maintained by the association.

d.	The total amount of money held by the association as reserves.

e.	If the statement is being furnished by the association, a statement as to whether the records of the association reflect any alterations or improvements to the unit that violate the declaration. The association is not obligated to provide information regarding alterations or improvements that occurred more than six years before the proposed sale. Nothing in this subdivision relieves the seller of a unit from the obligation to disclose alterations or improvements to the unit that violate the declaration, nor precludes the association from taking action against the purchaser of a unit for violations that are apparent at the time of purchase and that are not reflected in the association's records.

f.	If the statement is being furnished by the member, a statement as to whether the member has any knowledge of any alterations or improvements to the unit that violate the declaration.

g.	A statement of case names and case numbers for pending litigation with respect to the unit filed by the association against the member or filed by the member against the association.

The member shall not be required to disclose information concerning such pending litigation that would violate any applicable rule of attorney-client privilege under Arizona law.

    h.  A statement that provides "I hereby acknowledge that the declaration, bylaws and rules of the association constitute a contract between the association and me (the purchaser). By signing this statement, I acknowledge that I have read and understand the association's contract with me (the purchaser). I also understand that as a matter of Arizona law, if I fail to pay my association assessments, the association may foreclose on my property." The statement shall also include a signature line for the purchaser and shall be returned to the association within fourteen calendar days.

4.  A copy of the current operating budget of the association.

5.  A copy of the most recent annual financial report of the association. If the report is more than ten pages, the association may provide a summary of the report in lieu of the entire report.

6.  A copy of the most recent reserve study of the association, if any.

7.  A statement summarizing any pending lawsuits, except those relating to the collection of assessments owed by members other than the selling member, in which the association is a named party, including the amount of any money claimed.

B.  A purchaser or seller who is damaged by the failure of the member or the association to disclose the information required by subsection A of this section may pursue all remedies at law or in equity against the member or the association, whichever failed to comply with subsection A of this section, including the recovery of reasonable attorney fees.

C.  The association may charge the member a fee of no more than an aggregate of four hundred dollars to compensate the association for the costs incurred in the preparation of a statement or other documents furnished by the association pursuant to this section for purposes of resale disclosure, lien estoppel and any other services related to the transfer or use of the property. In addition, the association may charge a rush fee of no more than one hundred dollars if the rush services are required to be performed within seventy-two hours after the request for rush services, and may charge a statement or other documents update fee of no more than fifty dollars if thirty days or more have passed since the date of the original disclosure statement or the date the documents were delivered.

The association shall make available to any interested party the amount of any fee established from time to time by the association. If the aggregate fee for purposes of resale disclosure, lien estoppel and any other services related to the transfer or use of a property is less than four hundred dollars on January 1, 2010, the fee may increase at a rate of no more than twenty per cent per year based on the immediately preceding fiscal year's amount not to exceed the four hundred dollar aggregate fee. The association may charge the same fee without regard to whether the association is furnishing the statement or other documents in paper or electronic format.

D. The fees prescribed by this section shall be collected no earlier than at the close of escrow and may only be charged once to a member for that transaction between the parties specified in the notice required pursuant to subsection A of this section. An association shall not charge or collect a fee relating to services for resale disclosure, lien estoppel and any other services related to the transfer or use of a property except as specifically authorized in this section. An association that charges or collects a fee in violation of this section is subject to a civil penalty of no more than one thousand two hundred dollars.

E. This section applies to a managing agent for an association that is acting on behalf of the association.

F. The following are exempt from this section:
1. A sale in which a public report is issued pursuant to sections 32-2183 and 32-2197.02.
2. A sale pursuant to section 32-2181.02.
3. A conveyance by recorded deed that bears an exemption listed in section 11-1134, subsection B, paragraph 3 or 7. On recordation of the deed and for no additional charge, the member shall provide the association with the changes in ownership including the member's name, billing address and phone number. Failure to provide the information shall not prevent the member from qualifying for the exemption pursuant to this section.

G. For the purposes of this section, unless the context otherwise requires, "member" means the seller of the unit title and excludes any real estate salesperson or real estate broker who is licensed under title 32, chapter 20 and who is acting as a salesperson or broker, any escrow agent who is licensed under title 6, chapter 7 and who is acting as an escrow agent and also excludes a trustee of a deed of trust who is selling the property in a trustee's sale pursuant to chapter 6.1 of this title.

## ARS 33-1806.01. Rental property; member and agent information; fee; disclosure

A. A member may use the member's property as a rental property unless prohibited in the declaration and shall use it in accordance with the declaration's rental time period restrictions.

B. A member may designate in writing a third party to act as the member's agent with respect to all association matters relating to the rental property, except for voting in association elections and serving on the board of directors. The member shall sign the written designation and shall provide a copy of the written designation to the association. On delivery of the written designation, the association is authorized to conduct all association business relating to the member's rental property through the designated agent. Any notice given by the association to a member's designated agent on any matter relating to the member's rental property constitutes notice to the member.

C.  Notwithstanding any provision in the community documents, on rental of a member's property an association shall not require a member or a member's agent to disclose any information regarding a tenant other than **the name and contact information for any adults occupying the property, the time period of the lease, including the beginning and ending dates of the tenancy, and a description and the license plate numbers of the tenants' vehicles.** If the planned community is an age restricted community, the member, the member's agent or the tenant shall show a government issued identification that bears a photograph and that confirms that the tenant meets the community's age restrictions or requirements.

D.  On request of an association or its managing agent for the disclosures prescribed in subsection C of this section, the managing agent or, if there is no managing agent, the association may charge a fee of not more than twenty-five dollars, which shall be paid within fifteen days after the postmarked request. The fee may be charged for each new tenancy for that property but may not be charged for a renewal of a lease. Except for the fee permitted by this subsection and fees related to the use of recreational facilities, the association or its managing agent shall not assess, levy or charge a fee or fine or otherwise impose a requirement on a member's rental property any differently than on an owner-occupied property in the association.

E.  Notwithstanding any provision in the community documents, the association is prohibited from doing any of the following:
1.  Requiring a member to provide the association with a copy of the tenant's rental application, credit report, lease agreement or rental contract or other personal information except as prescribed by this section. This paragraph does not prohibit the association from acquiring a credit report on a person in an attempt to collect a debt.

2. Requiring the tenant to sign a waiver or other document limiting the tenant's due process rights as a condition of the tenant's occupancy of the rental property.
3. Prohibiting or otherwise restricting a member from serving on the board of directors based on the member's not being an occupant of the property.
4. Imposing on a member or managing agent any fee, assessment, penalty or other charge in an amount greater than fifteen dollars for incomplete or late information regarding the information requested pursuant to subsection C of this section.

F. Any attempt by an association to exceed the fee, assessment, penalty or other charge authorized by subsection D or E of this section voids the fee, assessment, penalty or other charge authorized by subsection D or E of this section. This section does not prevent an association from complying with the housing for older persons act of 1995 (P.L. 104-76; 109 Stat. 787).

G. An owner may use a crime free addendum as part of a lease agreement. This section does not prohibit the owner's use of a crime free addendum.

H. This section does not prohibit and an association may lawfully enforce a provision in the community documents that restricts the residency of persons who are required to be registered pursuant to section 13-3821 and who are classified as level two or level three offenders.

I. An owner of rental property shall abate criminal activity as authorized in section 12-991.

## ARS 33-1807. Lien for assessments; priority; mechanics' and materialmen's liens
A. The association has a lien on a unit for any assessment levied against that unit from the time the assessment becomes due. The association's lien for assessments, for charges for late payment of those assessments,

for reasonable collection fees and for reasonable attorney fees and costs incurred with respect to those assessments may be foreclosed in the same manner as a mortgage on real estate but may be foreclosed only if the owner has been delinquent in the payment of monies secured by the lien, excluding reasonable collection fees, reasonable attorney fees and charges for late payment of and costs incurred with respect to those assessments, for a period of one year or in the amount of one thousand two hundred dollars or more, whichever occurs first. Fees, charges, late charges, monetary penalties and interest charged pursuant to section 33-1803, other than charges for late payment of assessments are not enforceable as assessments under this section. If an assessment is payable in installments, the full amount of the assessment is a lien from the time the first installment of the assessment becomes due. The association has a lien for fees, charges, late charges, other than charges for late payment of assessments, monetary penalties or interest charged pursuant to section 33-1803 after the entry of a judgment in a civil suit for those fees, charges, late charges, monetary penalties or interest from a court of competent jurisdiction and the recording of that judgment in the office of the county recorder as otherwise provided by law. The association's lien for monies other than for assessments, for charges for late payment of those assessments, for reasonable collection fees and for reasonable attorney fees and costs incurred with respect to those assessments may not be foreclosed and is effective only on conveyance of any interest in the real property.

B. A lien for assessments, for charges for late payment of those assessments, for reasonable collection fees and for reasonable attorney fees and costs incurred with respect to those assessments under this section is prior to all other liens, interests and encumbrances on a unit except:
   1. Liens and encumbrances recorded before the recordation of the declaration.
   2. A recorded first mortgage on the unit, a seller's interest in a first contract for sale pursuant to chapter 6, article 3 of this title on the

unit recorded prior to the lien arising pursuant to subsection A of this section or a recorded first deed of trust on the unit.

3. Liens for real estate taxes and other governmental assessments or charges against the unit.

C. Subsection B of this section does not affect the priority of mechanics' or materialmen's liens or the priority of liens for other assessments made by the association. The lien under this section is not subject to chapter 8 of this title.

D. Unless the declaration otherwise provides, if two or more associations have liens for assessments created at any time on the same real estate those liens have equal priority.

E. Recording of the declaration constitutes record notice and perfection of the lien for assessments, for charges for late payment of assessments, for reasonable collection fees and for reasonable attorney fees and costs incurred with respect to those assessments. Further recordation of any claim of lien for assessments under this section is not required.

F. A lien for an unpaid assessment is extinguished unless proceedings to enforce the lien are instituted within three years after the full amount of the assessment becomes due.

G. This section does not prohibit:
   1. Actions to recover amounts for which subsection A of this section creates a lien.
   2. An association from taking a deed in lieu of foreclosure.

H. A judgment or decree in any action brought under this section shall include costs and reasonable attorney fees for the prevailing party.

I. On written request, the association shall furnish to a lienholder, escrow agent, unit owner or person designated by a unit owner a statement setting forth the amount of any unpaid assessment against the unit. The association shall furnish the statement within ten days after receipt of the request, and the statement is binding on the association, the board of directors and every unit owner if the statement is requested by an escrow agency that is licensed pursuant to title 6, chapter 7. Failure to provide the statement to the escrow agent within the time provided for in this subsection shall extinguish any lien for any unpaid assessment then due.

J. Notwithstanding any provision in the community documents or in any contract between the association and a management company, unless the member directs otherwise, all payments received on a member's account shall be applied first to any unpaid assessments, for unpaid charges for late payment of those assessments, for reasonable collection fees and for unpaid attorney fees and costs incurred with respect to those assessments, in that order, with any remaining amounts applied next to other unpaid fees, charges and monetary penalties or interest and late charges on any of those amounts

## ARS 33-1808. Flag display; political signs; caution signs; for sale, rent or lease signs; political activities

A. Notwithstanding any provision in the community documents, an association shall not prohibit the outdoor front yard or backyard display of any of the following:

1. The American flag or an official or replica of a flag of the United States army, navy, air force, marine corps or coast guard by an association member on that member's property if the American flag or military flag is displayed in a manner consistent with the federal flag code (P.L. 94-344; 90 Stat. 810; 4 United States Code sections 4 through 10).

2. The POW/MIA flag.

3. The Arizona state flag.

4. An Arizona Indian nation's flag.

5. The Gadsden flag.

B. The association shall adopt reasonable rules and regulations regarding the placement and manner of display of the American flag, the military flag, the POW/MIA flag, the Arizona state flag, or an Arizona Indian nation's flag. The association rules may regulate the location and size of flagpoles, may limit the member to displaying no more than two flags at once and may limit the height of the flagpole to no more than the height of the rooftop of the member's home but shall not prohibit the installation of a flagpole in the front yard or backyard of the member's property.

C. Notwithstanding any provision in the community documents, an association shall not prohibit the indoor or outdoor display of a political sign by an association member on that member's property, except that an association may prohibit the display of political signs earlier than seventy-one days before the day of an election and later than three days after an election day. An association may regulate the size and number of political signs that may be placed on a member's property if the association's regulation is no more restrictive than any applicable city, town or county ordinance that regulates the size and number of political signs on residential property. If the city, town or county in which the property is located does not regulate the size and number of political signs on residential property, the association shall not limit the number of political signs, except that the maximum aggregate total dimensions of all political signs on a member's property shall not exceed nine square feet. For the purposes of this subsection, "political sign" means a sign that attempts to influence the outcome of an election, including supporting or opposing the recall of a public officer or supporting or opposing the circulation of a petition for a ballot measure, question or proposition or the recall of a public officer.

D. Notwithstanding any provision in the community documents, an association shall not prohibit the use of cautionary signs regarding children if the signs are used and displayed as follows:
1. The signs are displayed in residential areas only.

2. The signs are removed within one hour of children ceasing to play.
3. The signs are displayed only when children are actually present within fifty feet of the sign.
4. The temporary signs are no taller than three feet in height.
5. The signs are professionally manufactured or produced.

E. Notwithstanding any provision in the community documents, an association shall not prohibit children who reside in the planned community from engaging in recreational activity on residential roadways that are under the jurisdiction of the association and on which the posted speed limit is twenty-five miles per hour or less.

F. Notwithstanding any provision in the community documents, an association shall not prohibit or charge a fee for the use of, placement of or the indoor or outdoor display of a for sale, for rent or for lease sign and a sign rider by an association member on that member's property in any combination, including a sign that indicates the member is offering the property for sale by owner. The size of a sign offering a property for sale, for rent or for lease shall be in conformance with the industry standard size sign, which shall not exceed eighteen by twenty-four inches, and the industry standard size sign rider, which shall not exceed six by twenty-four inches. This subsection applies only to a commercially produced sign, and an association may prohibit the use of signs that are not commercially produced. With respect to real estate for sale, for rent or for lease in the planned community, an association shall not prohibit in any way other than as is specifically authorized by this section or otherwise regulate any of the following:

1. Temporary open house signs or a member's for sale sign. The association shall not require the use of particular signs indicating an open house or real property for sale and may not further regulate the use of temporary open house or for sale signs that are industry standard size and that are owned or used by the seller or the seller's agent.

2. Open house hours. The association may not limit the hours for an open house for real estate that is for sale in the planned community, except that the association may prohibit an open house being held before 8:00 a.m. or after 6:00 p.m. and may prohibit open house signs on the common areas of the planned community.

3. An owner's or an owner's agent's for rent or for lease sign unless an association's documents prohibit or restrict leasing of a member's property. An association shall not further regulate a for rent or for lease sign or require the use of a particular for rent or for lease sign other than the for rent or for lease sign shall not be any larger than the industry standard size sign of eighteen by twenty-four inches on or in the member's property. If rental or leasing of a member's property is not prohibited or restricted, the association may prohibit an open house for rental or leasing being held before 8:00 a.m. or after 6:00 p.m.

G. Notwithstanding any provision in the community documents, an association shall not prohibit door to door political activity, including solicitations of support or opposition regarding candidates or ballot issues, and shall not prohibit the circulation of political petitions, including candidate nomination petitions or petitions in support of or opposition to an initiative, referendum or recall or other political issue on property normally open to visitors within the association, except that an association may do the following:

1. Restrict or prohibit the door to door political activity from sunset to sunrise.

2. Require the prominent display of an identification tag for each person engaged in the activity, along with the prominent identification of the candidate or ballot issue that is the subject of the support or opposition.

H. A planned community shall not make any regulations regarding the number of candidates supported, the number of public officers supported or opposed in a recall or the number of propositions supported or opposed on a political sign.

I.  A planned community shall not require political signs to be commercially produced or professionally manufactured or prohibit the utilization of both sides of a political sign.

J.  A planned community is not required to comply with subsection G if the planned community restricts vehicular or pedestrian access to the planned community. Nothing in this section requires a planned community to make its common elements other than roadways and sidewalks that are normally open to visitors available for the circulation of political petitions to anyone who is not an owner or resident of the community.

K.  An association or managing agent that violates subsection F of this section forfeits and extinguishes the lien rights authorized under section 33-1807 against that member's property for a period of six consecutive months from the date of the violation.

### 33-1809. Parking; public service and public safety emergency vehicles; definition

A.  Notwithstanding any provision in the community documents, an association shall not prohibit a resident from parking a motor vehicle on a street or driveway in the planned community if the vehicle is required to be available at designated periods at the person's residence as a condition of the person's employment and either of the following applies:

1.  The resident is employed by a public service corporation that is regulated by the corporation commission, an entity regulated by the federal energy regulatory commission or a municipal utility and the public service corporation or municipal utility is required to prepare for emergency deployments of personnel and equipment for repair or maintenance of natural gas, electrical,

telecommunications or water infrastructure, the vehicle has a gross vehicle weight rating of twenty thousand pounds or less and is owned or operated by the public service corporation or municipal utility and the vehicle bears an official emblem or other visible designation of the public service corporation or municipal utility.

2. The resident is employed by a public safety agency, including police or fire service for a federal, state, local or tribal agency or a private fire service provider or an ambulance service provider that is regulated pursuant to title 36, chapter 21.1, and the vehicle has a gross vehicle weight rating of ten thousand pounds or less and bears an official emblem or other visible designation of that agency.

B. For the purposes of this section, "telecommunications" means the transmission of information of the user's choosing between or among points specified by the user without change in the form or content of the information as sent and received. Telecommunications does not include commercial mobile radio services.

### ARS 33-1810. Board of directors; annual audit

Unless any provision in the planned community documents requires an annual audit by a certified public accountant, the board of directors shall provide for an annual financial audit, review or compilation of the association. The audit, review or compilation shall be completed no later than one hundred eighty days after the end of the association's fiscal year and shall be made available upon request to the members within thirty days after its completion.

### ARS 33-1812. Proxies; absentee ballots; definition

A. Notwithstanding any provision in the community documents, after termination of the period of declarant control, votes allocated to a unit may not be cast pursuant to a proxy. The association shall provide for votes to be cast in person and by absentee ballot and, in addition, the association may provide for voting by some other form of delivery, including the use of e-mail and fax delivery. Notwithstanding section

10-3708 or the provisions of the community documents, any action taken at an annual, regular or special meeting of the members shall comply with all of the following if absentee ballots or ballots provided by some other form of delivery are used:

1. The ballot shall set forth each proposed action.
2. The ballot shall provide an opportunity to vote for or against each proposed action.
3. The ballot is valid for only one specified election or meeting of the members and expires automatically after the completion of the election or meeting.
4. The ballot specifies the time and date by which the ballot must be delivered to the board of directors in order to be counted, which shall be at least seven days after the date that the board delivers the unvoted ballot to the member.
5. The ballot does not authorize another person to cast votes on behalf of the member.
6. The completed ballot and envelope and any related materials shall contain the name, address and signature of the person voting, except that if the community documents permit secret ballots, only the envelope and any nonballot-related materials shall contain the name, address and signature of the voter.
7. Ballots, envelopes and related materials, including sign-in sheets if used, shall be retained in electronic or paper format and made available for member inspection for at least one year after completion of the election.

B. Votes cast by absentee ballot or other form of delivery, including the use of e-mail and fax delivery, are valid for the purpose of establishing a quorum.

C. Notwithstanding subsection A of this section, an association for a timeshare plan as defined in section 32-2197 may permit votes by a proxy that is duly executed by a unit owner.

D. For the purposes of this section, "period of declarant control" means the time during which the declarant or persons designated by the declarant may elect or appoint the members of the board of directors pursuant to the community documents or by virtue of superior voting power.

### ARS 33-1814. Slum property; professional management

For any residential rental units that have been declared a slum property by the city or town pursuant to section 33-1905 and that are in the planned community, the association is responsible for enforcing any requirement for a licensed property management firm that is imposed by a city or town pursuant to section 33-1906.

### ARS 33-1815. Association authority; commercial signage

Notwithstanding any provision in the community documents, after an association has approved a commercial sign, including its registered trademark that is located on properties zoned for commercial use in the planned community, the association, including any subsequently elected board of directors, may not revoke or modify its approval of that sign if the owner or operator of the sign has received approval for the sign from the local or county governing body with jurisdiction over the sign.

### ARS 33-1816. Solar energy devices; reasonable restrictions; fees and costs

A. Notwithstanding any provision in the community documents, an association shall not prohibit the installation or use of a solar energy device as defined in section 44-1761.

B. An association may adopt reasonable rules regarding the placement of a solar energy device if those rules do not prevent the installation, impair the functioning of the device or restrict its use or adversely affect the cost or efficiency of the device.

C.  Notwithstanding any provision of the community documents, the court shall award reasonable attorney fees and costs to any party who substantially prevails in an action against the board of directors of the association for a violation of this section.

## ARS 33-1817. Declaration amendment; design, architectural committees; review

A.  Except during the period of declarant control, or if during the period of declarant control with the written consent of the declarant in each instance, the following apply to an amendment to a declaration:

1.  The declaration may be amended by the association, if any, or, if there is no association or board, the owners of the property that is subject to the declaration, by an affirmative vote or written consent of the number of owners or eligible voters specified in the declaration, including the assent of any individuals or entities that are specified in the declaration.

2.  An amendment to a declaration may apply to fewer than all of the lots or less than all of the property that is bound by the declaration and an amendment is deemed to conform to the general design and plan of the community, if both of the following apply:

    a.  The amendment receives the affirmative vote or written consent of the number of owners or eligible voters specified in the declaration, including the assent of any individuals or entities that are specified in the declaration.

    b.  The amendment receives the affirmative vote or written consent of all of the owners of the lots or property to which the amendment applies.

3.  Within thirty days after the adoption of any amendment pursuant to this section, the association or, if there is no association or board, an owner that is authorized by the affirmative vote on or the written consent to the amendment shall prepare, execute and record a written instrument setting forth the amendment.

4.  Notwithstanding any provision in the declaration that provides for periodic renewal of the declaration, an amendment to the

declaration is effective immediately on recordation of the instrument in the county in which the property is located.

B. Notwithstanding any provision in the community documents:
1. Membership on a design review committee, an architectural committee or a committee that performs similar functions, however denominated, for the planned community shall include at least one member of the board of directors who shall serve as chairperson of the committee.
2. For new construction of the main residential structure on a lot or for rebuilds of the main residential structure on a lot and only in a planned community that has enacted design guidelines, architectural guidelines or other similar rules, however denominated, and if the association documents permit the association to charge the member a security deposit and the association requires the member to pay a security deposit to secure completion of the member's construction project or compliance with approved plans, all of the following apply:
   a. The deposit shall be placed in a trust account with the following instructions:
      i. The cost of the trust account shall be shared equally between the association and the member.
      ii. If the construction project is abandoned, the board of directors may determine the appropriate use of any deposit monies.
      iii. Any interest earned on the refundable security deposit shall become part of the security deposit.
   b. The association or the design review committee must hold a final design approval meeting for the purpose of issuing approval of the plans, and the member or member's agent must have the opportunity to attend the meeting. If the plans are approved, the association's design review representative shall provide written acknowledgement that the approved plans, including any approved amendments, are in compliance with

all rules and guidelines in effect at the time of the approval and that the refund of the deposit requires that construction be completed in accordance with those approved plans.

c. The association must provide for at least two on-site formal reviews during construction for the purpose of determining compliance with the approved plans. The member or member's agent shall be provided the opportunity to attend both formal reviews. Within five business days after the formal reviews, the association shall cause a written report to be provided to the member or member's agent specifying any deficiencies, violations or unapproved variations from the approved plans, as amended, that have come to the attention of the association.

d. Within thirty business days after the second formal review, the association shall provide to the member a copy of the written report specifying any deficiencies, violations or unapproved variations from the approved plans, as amended, that have come to the attention of the association. If the written report does not specify any deficiencies, violations or unapproved variations from the approved plans, as amended, that have come to the attention of the association, the association shall promptly release the deposit monies to the member. If the report identifies any deficiencies, violations or unapproved variations from the approved plans, as amended, the association may hold the deposit for one hundred eighty days or until receipt of a subsequent report of construction compliance, whichever is less. If a report of construction compliance is received before the one hundred eightieth day, the association shall promptly release the deposit monies to the member. If a compliance report is not received within one hundred eighty days, the association shall release the deposit monies promptly from the trust account to the association.

e. Neither the approval of the plans nor the approval of the actual construction by the association or the design review committee shall constitute a representation or warranty that the plans or construction comply with applicable governmental requirements or applicable engineering, design or safety standards. The association in its discretion may release all or any part of the deposit to the member before receiving a compliance report. Release of the deposit to the member does not constitute a representation or warranty from the association that the construction complies with the approved plans.

3. Approval of a construction project's architectural designs, plans and amendments shall not unreasonably be withheld.

## ARS 33-1818. Community authority over public roadways; applicability

A. Notwithstanding any provision in the community documents, after the period of declarant control, an association has no authority over and shall not regulate any roadway for which the ownership has been dedicated to or is otherwise held by a governmental entity.

B. This section applies only to those planned communities for which the declaration is recorded after December 31, 2014.

# State and City Laws

Below are the home-based business laws for the State of Arizona and the Town of Gilbert, AZ. Below the laws will be my comments and discussion of an example of conflicting laws and which laws trump the others.

## ARS 11-820 State Home-based Business Law

A. Any ordinance authorized by this chapter shall not restrict or otherwise regulate the owner of a home-based business that holds a valid license from:

1. Making residential property improvements to add doors, shelving or display racks for use by the home-based business.

2. Displaying a temporary commercial sign on the residential property during business hours, if the sign is not more than twentyfour inches by twentyfour inches.
3. Selling or offering for sale any goods.
4. Generating traffic, parking or delivery activity that does not cause on-street parking congestion or a substantial increase in traffic through the residential area.
5. Having more than one client on the property at one time.
6. Employing any of the following:
    a. Residents of the primary dwelling.
    b. Immediate family members.
    c. One or two individuals who are not residents of the primary dwelling or immediate family members.

B. This section does not preclude a county from imposing reasonable operating requirements on a home-based business or a residential property used by a home-based business.

C. For the purposes of this section:
1. "Goods" means any merchandise, equipment, products, supplies or materials.
2. "Home-based business" means any business for the limited manufacture, provision or sale of goods or services that is owned and operated by the owner or tenant of the residential property.
3. "Immediate family member" means a spouse, child, sibling, parent, grandparent, grandchild, stepparent, stepchild or stepsibling whether related by adoption or blood.
4. "License" means any permit, certificate, approval, registration, charter or similar form of authorization that is required by law and that is issued by any agency, department, board or commission of this state or of any political subdivision of this state for the purpose of operating a business in this state or to an individual who provides a service to any person and the license is required to perform that service.

## Home Occupation Guidelines, Gilbert, Arizona

- A Business License is required for all home-based businesses.
- A home occupation use may only be conducted within the dwelling unit or an accessory structure and must be incidental to the principal use of the dwelling unit for residential purposes.
- Other than family members residing within the dwelling unit, there shall be no more than one full-time employee working at a home occupation.
- There shall be no signs, display of merchandise or products in trade, outdoor storage of materials or any other exterior indication of a home occupation.
- A home occupation use shall not produce noise, odors, vibrations, glare, dust, fumes or electrical interference.
- The use and/or storage of any flammable or toxic chemicals except for normal household usage, is prohibited.
- A home occupation use shall not generate vehicular or truck traffic in greater volume than normally expected in the residential district.
- All parking for the home occupation use shall be on-site and comply with LDC Article 4.2: Off-Street Parking and Loading Regulations.
- At no time shall the property in which a home occupation use is located be used as a headquarters for the assembly of employees for instruction or other purposes, including dispatch to other locations.
- All home-based businesses shall complete a Wastewater Questionnaire.
- Business Licenses are reviewed on a case to case basis.

## My Comments

As was stated earlier, in addition to the non-profit corporation and planned community laws there are state and local county or city laws that associations must be aware of. The state of Arizona home-based business law, 11-820, is one that would apply to HOA's. What this law says, in sub section A, is that any ordinance (by local city or town jurisdictions) <u>shall not restrict</u> the owner of a home-based business — *that holds a valid license* — from doing certain things that are listed in the section.

The following example is for the state of Arizona, the Town of Gilbert, and a hypothetical HOA in Gilbert.

- The HOA rules are that only certain signs are permitted. A home-based business sign is not on the permitted sign list.
- The Town of Gilbert home-based business guidelines state in paragraph 4, *"There shall be no signs, display of merchandise or products in trade, outdoor storage of materials or any other exterior indication of a home occupation."*
- The Arizona state law ARS 11-820 as revised to become effective in August, 2017 states in paragraph 2, that *"any ordinance authorized by this chapter <u>shall not restrict</u> or otherwise regulate the owner of a home-based business that holds a valid license from…"* *"2. Displaying a temporary commercial sign on the residential property during business hours, if the sign is not more than twenty-four inches by twenty-four inches."…*

Here's the conflict:

- The HOA restricts a home-based business from having a sign on the property.
- The Town of Gilbert restricts a home-based business from having a sign on the property.
- The Arizona state law doesn't allow a City to restrict a home-based business from having a sign with a maximum size of 24" x 24" during business hours.

The state is the highest authority so they trump the city and the HOA. Therefore, according to my layperson interpretation of those laws, a home-based business in an HOA can have a 24" x 24" commercial sign during business hours.

Is my opinion correct? I think so, but I'm not an attorney. My point in using this example is this:

Each director should be familiar with the laws that govern HOA's so that when questions like this come up, they know where to look for the answer. When a director does the research and finds that the HOA rules appear to be in conflict with the local or state laws, he or she should bring this to the attention of the board. The board should then present the information to the association attorney who can provide a legal opinion on the issue, and if necessary, the rules can be amended accordingly.

A good practice for any board would be to establish a Rules Committee who, beginning in June of each year when the legislative session is over, would review all of the association rules and compare them with the non-profit corporation laws, planned community laws, state laws, and local ordinances so that by August, when the new laws become effective, a draft of recommended rules amendments would be ready to present to the board for review and approval.

CHAPTER 5

# DIRECTORS AND OFFICERS DUTIES

## CHARACTERISTICS OF A GOOD BOARD MEMBER

Before we proceed to the directors' and officers' duties, let's first discuss what characteristics a good board member should have.

### Good character
A person with good character is likely to be known to have attributes such as courage, loyalty, and fortitude that promote good habits. Character also describes who we are as a person, and influences the daily choices we make.

### Strong integrity
Integrity is that quality of being honest and having strong moral principles. It is the desire to uphold a high degree of moral and ethical standards.

### Calm judgment
Directors are leaders of the community, and as such they need to have the ability to remain calm under pressure. A leader should not exhibit visible

tension when placed under stress. This attribute is similarly necessary for an airline pilot. A pilot must exhibit calmness in talking to her passengers when the airplane is experiencing difficulties and she is under a high degree of stress while attempting to solve the airplane problem. A board member must do the same.

### Willingness to serve

It should go without saying that a good director needs to be willing to donate her time to do the volunteer work that goes along with being a board member. The director should know that it is a thankless job, and be willing to accept criticism when it is levied by community members who may be unhappy with a decision the board has made.

### Committed to the best interests of the community as a whole

A director must place the interest of the association above his or her own interests. When dealing with the desires of community members, there may be a small group of members who want something in the community that is costly, yet is not beneficial to the majority. A director must be able to recognize and make decisions that serve the best interests of the majority of the community and to reject projects that benefit only a few.

### Relevant experience or background

It certainly helps if the director has a business background and/or has had the experience of serving on boards in the past.

### Strong people skills

In serving on an HOA board, a director will deal with many different personalities in occasionally hotly debated subjects, sometimes in a charged atmosphere. It helps if he or she has the knowledge and ability to communicate effectively with these different personality types in order to maintain reason and order in board meetings.

# DIRECTORS DUTIES

In addition to the fiduciary duties found in the non-profit corporation laws, the duties of the directors are usually spelled out in the association Bylaws. Below is a sample list of directors' duties. Most are boilerplate paragraphs that many attorneys' use, with possible modifications, and that may be found in any number of association's Bylaws.

Duties. It shall be the duty of the Board of Directors to:

- Supervise all officers, agents and employees of the Association, and to see that their duties are properly performed; and
- cause to be kept a complete record of all of its acts and corporate affairs; and
- fix the amount of the annual assessment against each lot at least thirty (30) days in advance of each annual assessment period; and
- take such action, as and when the board deems such action appropriate, but after notice as provided in the declaration, to foreclose the lien against any property for which assessments are not paid and/or to bring an action at law against the member personally obligated to pay the same;
- procure and maintain adequate liability and hazard insurance on the general common area and assets owned by the Association;
- cause all officers or employees having fiscal responsibilities to be bonded, as it may deem appropriate;
- cause the maintenance responsibilities of the Association set forth in the declaration to be performed.

# OFFICERS DUTIES

Below is a sample of officers' duties that are usually spelled out in an association's Bylaws:

*President:*

- Is the official spokesperson for the association.
- Chairs all of the board meetings.
- Sees that orders and resolutions of the board are carried out.
- Sets the community vision.
- Prioritizes goals.
- Encourages volunteers to join committees.
- Determines the agenda after receiving other director requests.
- Assists treasurer with budget.
- Oversees committee work.

*Vice President:*

- Acts in place of the president when the president is absent.
- Performs any other duties required by the board.
- Must be kept informed of all issues the president is dealing with so that he or she can step in and do the job when the president is absent.

*Secretary:*

- Keeps the minutes and records the votes of all meetings.
- Sees that the association history is preserved.
- Maintains the association records.

*Treasurer:*

- Is the financial voice of the board.
- Receives and deposits all monies into the appropriate bank account.
- Liaison to the financial advisers.
- Shall cause an annual audit of the association books.

- Prepares the annual budget, balance sheet and P&L for the annual membership meeting.
- Works with reserve specialists for the reserve study program.

## *Delegation:*

- A board may delegate the officers duties to a manager or managing agent, however,
- the board may not delegate its responsibilities. (*The buck still stops with the board.*)

# RULES ENFORCEMENT

## *Rules Amendments*

The board is given many powers, and one is the power to develop rules and regulations. Those rules can be used to explain and clarify the covenants in the CC&R's but cannot add to, modify, or delete them.

Since laws change annually, rules also should be amended annually in order to make sure they comply with new laws.

The board can delegate the duty to amend rules to a manager. However, HOA attorney Jonathan Olcott states that he has never seen that done, and it would be a horrible practice to delegate 100% of that duty to anyone. He went on to say that it is a total abdication of the directors' duty to the corporation.

In my personal opinion, it would be acceptable for the manager, or as discussed earlier, a committee, to draft the changes and

present the new law and the proposed rules amendment draft to the board for approval.

A good practice would be for the manager or committee to have a reminder system set up on a calendar so that each year at the time the legislative session ends, the board will know that it's time to check for any newly passed laws that affect the association, and the date they become effective.

# DIRECTION AND VISION

## *Putting Out Fires, or Preventing Them?*

- Is your board continuously putting out fires?
- Is there one crisis after another?
- Is there in-fighting among directors?
- Is there a parade of complaints from association members?

If the answer is yes, then perhaps the board should implement changes that will prevent fires before they begin. These suggestions may help:

- Listen objectively.
- Respect everyone's opinion.
- Investigate all complaints.
- Take positive action to solve problems.
- Put procedures in place to prevent recurrences.
- Form an Oversight Committee.

### *Listen Actively*

Any time an association member or board member expresses their opinion, others should be listening carefully instead of thinking of what they want to say next. One should listen carefully in order to fully understand what the speaker is trying to convey. When we listen carefully and objectively, we may discover that our own opinion is not too different from the speakers' opinion. In that case, it may be easier than we thought to negotiate a middle ground that's acceptable to everyone.

### Respect Others' Opinions

The reason a board consists of more than one person (usually from five to eleven directors) is that boards comprised of several individuals provides the community with the benefit of having input from varying viewpoints. Through the negotiation process a board will normally end up with a decision that is better than any one person's idea. This is synergy at work, where the whole is greater than the sum of the parts.

Every director has a right to his or her own opinion and the right to express that opinion, as long as it is expressed in accordance with the rules of meeting decorum. (*The sub chapter "Meeting Decorum" can be found in Chapter 7.*) While everyone has the right to have different opinions, the opinions of others must be treated with respect.

Directors must listen to and respect other director's opinions, even if they disagree, and equally important, directors must actively listen to community members. In a community of thousands of homeowners, and a board of five to eleven directors, there will no doubt be complaints from time to time that the board must address. Every complaint, no matter how small, should be listened to very carefully, investigated, and resolved.

### Investigate

One situation I became aware of is where a community member would make frequent complaints to the board about the maintenance status of some of the common amenities. One complaint was that several of the electrical boxes at the base of light poles were missing cover plates, leaving bare wires hanging out of the box, thus creating potential fire and shock hazards. The manager responded that those issues had been taken care of.

The same complaints were repeated for several months, causing one board member to investigate and discover that the manager was in error. The wires were hanging out of the box just as the member had reported, and there were other maintenance issues as well. The board member reported his findings to the manager and the items were subsequently corrected. Had the board listened actively and investigated the complaints immediately, they may have put that fire out early.

## Take Positive (Not Negative) Action

Any time there is a problem, it is best to attempt to solve the problem with positive action rather than taking an adversarial approach. There are some HOA attorneys who advocate taking a strong adversarial approach and effectively use what I would term a bullying approach to address an issue. But does bullying solve an issue long term?

An adversarial approach to solving problems with neighbors, whether they are directors on the board or community members, will almost always create ill feelings, and in many cases may involve some degree of legal action against the association. Whereas, taking positive action prior to any adversarial action is more likely to result in a long term solution to the problem.

## Oversight Committee

In my opinion, boards are well advised to create an "Oversight Committee." As you've read in the sub chapter "Directors Duties," the board is responsible to supervise all agents and employees to see that their work is properly performed. In many large associations there will be an in-house manager hired directly by the board. Smaller associations will hire a management company who will assign a manager to deal with some of the day-to-day business of the association.

No matter if the manager is in-house or assigned by a management company, the board must see that their work is being performed properly. If the board establishes an Oversight Committee, that committee would be charged with performing certain periodic inspections of the association property to ensure that scheduled preventative maintenance is being performed, and that contracted work is being performed properly, and report back to the board on a monthly or quarterly basis.

The purpose of the committee would not be to micro-manage the manager. The committee would simply report its observations back to the board along with any recommendations they feel appropriate. The board could discuss the report, and if work is not being performed properly, the manager would have the opportunity to offer an explanation, and be instructed to take appropriate action to solve any issue(s).

## Charter Club Committee

In 2016, I was assigned to a committee consisting of four members to develop a set of rules for the existing Charter Clubs in our master association. Charter Clubs are social clubs organized for a specific purpose, such as a Tennis Club, Golf Club, Women's Club, Senior's Club, Bocce Ball Club, etc. By being an organized club sanctioned by the association, there are certain rules the clubs must follow. The benefit for clubs is that they are able to reserve meeting rooms on an annual basis for some of their activities, plus other benefits.

Developing a set of Charter Club rules was a daunting challenge because none of us knew where to start. I began searching the Internet for "charter club rules" to get some ideas on how to proceed, and, fortunately, found a set of charter rules developed by the Del Webb Corporation. Their rules consisted of about 65 pages, which was considerably more than our HOA would ever need. So, I went through the document and immediately eliminated about 30 pages we would never need.

At our first committee meeting, I presented the reduced document to the committee, suggesting that we use it as a template that we could modify to meet the needs of our HOA. In addition to the template, we had to consider several attorney opinions on how the clubs should be organized.

The members of this committee were all familiar with HOA operation, and had previous experience working on committees. One was a former board member, and two, including myself, were current board members. We were all independent thinkers and willing to voice our opinion — a good thing. But even better, each member was willing to actively listen to the other members' opinions and treat them with respect, even as we disagreed with some of the opinions. When four people are willing to work together like that, a lot of progress can be made in a relatively short period of time.

Our first challenge was how do we proceed, where do we begin? The issue of how to proceed was a lively debate, and, in fact, all through the process there was lively debate. One person would throw out an idea or suggestion, and someone else would throw out a different idea. We sometimes had four ideas to debate on one issue. Each person would be allowed to elaborate on his or her position while the others listened.

As a result, the decisions were a compilation of all members' ideas. While each committee member would win some and lose some debates, we joked about it, and didn't think of it in terms of losing anything; instead, we thought of it as a successful step toward the completion of the Charter Club rules.

After determining our course of action, we began studying the legal opinions for comprehension, and in some cases, had to debate the intent of the attorney regarding certain recommendations.

When we began work on the Del Webb document that we were using as a template, we decided to go through the document line by line, eliminating everything that did not apply to our HOA, and adding language necessary for our clubs. Every addition needed to comply with the legal opinions.

Through tough but respectful debate, this committee used a 30 page document as a template and developed a 12 page set of Charter Club rules designed especially for social clubs in our HOA. The finished product bore no resemblance to the original Del Webb document.

# CHAPTER 6

# REMOVAL OF DIRECTORS AND OFFICERS

## REMOVAL OF A DIRECTOR

The removal of a director often is built on a misunderstanding of the law; there have been conflicts over this topic that probably cost associations a lot of money in legal fees. Therefore, every board member and anyone contemplating becoming a board member should understand this topic in order to avoid placing the association and individual directors at legal risk.

By understanding this law, and some of the other laws taken as a whole, a board can recognize when they are receiving erroneous advice from an attorney.

There is a procedure in Title 10-3808 for removing a director, but the procedure shown below in Title 33-1813 trumps Title 10-3808. If the members of a planned community wish to remove a board member, they need to use ARS 33-1813. The removal of a director is serious business and should only be undertaken under the guidance of an attorney. As soon as community members deliver to the association a petition to remove a director, the clock starts, and events must happen within certain time frames. Therefore, the association must have their attorney's advice and guidance throughout the entire process.

To be clear, only association members can remove a director from the board, unless there is an exception in the Bylaws. Since the board did not elect directors, it cannot remove one. As you read this law, you'll see that it has very specific procedures that must be followed, and if something is missed, the recall may be challenged as illegal; that's why it's imperative that an attorney guide the association anytime the removal of a director is contemplated.

Let's look at the planned community law and learn how members can legally remove a director.

### ARS 33-1813. Removal of board member; special meeting

A. Notwithstanding any provision of the declaration or bylaws to the contrary, all of the following apply to a meeting at which a member of the board of directors, other than a member appointed by the declarant, is proposed to be removed from the board of directors:

1. The members of the association who are eligible to vote at the time of the meeting may remove any member of the board of directors, other than a member appointed by the declarant, by a majority vote of those voting on the matter at a meeting of the members.

2. The meeting of the members shall be called pursuant to this section and action may be taken only if a quorum is present.

3. The members of the association may remove any member of the board of directors with or without cause, other than a member appointed by the declarant.

4. For purposes of calling for removal of a member of the board of directors, other than a member appointed by the declarant, the following apply:

   a. In an association with one thousand or fewer members, on receipt of a petition that calls for removal of a member of the board of directors and that is signed by the number of persons who are eligible to vote in the association at the time the person signs the petition equal to at least twenty-five percent of the votes in the association or by the number of persons who are eligible to vote in the association at the time the person signs the petition equal to at least one hundred votes in the association, whichever is less, the board shall call and provide written notice of a special meeting of the association as prescribed by section 33-1804, subsection B.

b.  Notwithstanding section 33-1804, subsection B, in an association with more than one thousand members, on receipt of a petition that calls for removal of a member of the board of directors and that is signed by the number of persons who are eligible to vote in the association at the time the person signs the petition equal to at least ten percent of the votes in the association or by the number of persons who are eligible to vote in the association at the time the person signs the petition equal to at least one thousand votes in the association, whichever is less, the board shall call and provide written notice of a special meeting of the association. The board shall provide written notice of a special meeting as prescribed by section 33-1804, subsection B.

c.  The special meeting shall be called, noticed and held within thirty days after receipt of the petition.

d.  For purposes of a special meeting called pursuant to this subsection, a quorum is present if the number of owners who are eligible to vote in the association at the time the person attends the meeting equal to at least twenty percent of the votes of the association or the number of persons who are eligible to vote in the association at the time the person attends the meeting equal to at least one thousand votes, whichever is less, is present at the meeting in person or as otherwise permitted by law.

e.  If a civil action is filed regarding the removal of a board member, the prevailing party in the civil action shall be awarded its reasonable attorney fees and costs.

f.  The board of directors shall retain all documents and other records relating to the proposed removal of the member of the board of directors and any election or other action taken for that director's replacement for at least one year after the date of the special meeting and shall permit members to inspect those documents and records pursuant to section 33-1805.

g.  A petition that calls for the removal of the same member of the board of directors shall not be submitted more than once during each term of office for that member.

5.  On removal of at least one but fewer than a majority of the members of the board of directors at a special meeting of the membership called pursuant to this subsection, the vacancies shall be filled as provided in the community documents.

6.  On removal of a majority of the members of the board of directors at a special meeting of the membership called pursuant to this subsection, or if the community documents do not provide a method for filling board vacancies, the association shall hold an election for the replacement of the removed directors at a separate meeting of the members of the association that is held not later than thirty days after the meeting at which the members of the board of directors were removed.

7.  A member of the board of directors who is removed pursuant to this subsection is not eligible to serve on the board of directors again until after the expiration of the removed board member's term of office, unless the community documents specifically provide for a longer period of ineligibility.

B.  For an association in which board members are elected from separately designated voting districts, a member of the board of directors, other than a member appointed by the declarant, may be removed only by a vote of the members from that voting district, and only the members from that voting district are eligible to vote on the matter or be counted for purposes of determining a quorum.

### Removal of an Officer

In Arizona, the removal of an officer is not addressed in Title 33, although it may be addressed in your Bylaws, therefore, one should look to your Bylaws and Title 10 to find that information.

In ARS 10-3843 B, it states that the board can remove an officer at any time, with or without cause.

Below is the law:

### ARS 10-3843. Resignation and removal of officers

A.  An officer may resign at any time by delivering notice to the corporation. A resignation is effective when the notice is delivered unless the notice specifies a later effective date or event. If a resignation is made effective at a later date or event and the corporation accepts the later effective date, its board of directors may fill the pending vacancy before the effective date if the board of directors provides that the successor does not take office until the effective date.

B.  A board of directors may remove any officer at any time with or without cause.

CHAPTER 7

# CONDUCTING MEETINGS

## TYPES OF MEETINGS

In an HOA there are two types of meetings:

- Members Meetings
- Board of Directors Meetings

### Members Meetings

Member meetings are typically held once each year. This meeting is usually where new board members are elected. There will also be a report on accomplishments during the year, and possibly a discussion of what the board plans to accomplish in the following year. It is not a board meeting; no association business issues are to be discussed. It is the "members" meeting and is the time for members to voice their opinions, concerns, and desires for the community.

The Bylaws will usually state how often a Members Meeting must be held; with most associations it is probably every 12 to 14 months.

The Bylaws will also state what constitutes a quorum for the Members Meeting. Usually it is 1/10 of the votes of the membership who are present in person or by absentee ballot. If there are 1,000 membership votes, then 100 attending in person or sending in an absentee ballot is a quorum.

### Special Members Meetings

The President, the board, or 1/10th of the membership can call for a Special Members Meeting.

### Board of Directors Regular Meetings

Regular meetings of the board of directors are for discussion and action on association business. The Bylaws will determine how often the board must meet, although in many cases the Bylaws allow the board to determine how often they are to meet. Boards in small communities may have such a small volume of business to conduct that they may meet quarterly. The boards of larger communities may need to meet monthly in order to take care of the volume of anticipated business.

### Special Board Meetings

The President or two members of the board may call a Special Board Meeting for business that can't wait until the next regular board meeting. Forty-eight hours' notice of the meeting must be given to all directors, and the purpose of the meeting must be stated. The minutes of the special meeting must be read into the minutes of the next regular board meeting.

### Emergency Board Meetings

In Arizona, ARS 33-1804 E 3 provides that "an emergency meeting of the board of directors may be called to discuss business or take action that cannot be delayed for the fortyeight hours required for notice. The minutes of the emergency meeting shall state the reason necessitating the emergency meeting. The board of directors may act only on emergency matters at that emergency meeting and may not take action on non-emergency matters. The minutes of the emergency meeting shall be read and approved at the next regularly scheduled meeting of the board of directors."

# Quorum

A discussion about meetings wouldn't be complete without defining what is meant by a quorum.

If you look in Robert's Rules of Order, you'll see that a quorum is defined as the *"…minimum number of voting members who must be present at a properly called meeting in order to conduct business.…"*

There are two types of main meetings in an HOA that will require a quorum, and the Association Bylaws should state the quorum for each:

- Members Meeting, and
- Board of Directors Meeting

**Members Meeting**: Let's say that an Associations' Bylaws require 1/10 of the members to be present either in person or by absentee ballot to constitute a quorum. In a community of 1,000 homes, assuming every member is entitled to vote, 100 members would have to be present either in person or by submitting an absentee ballot in order to have a quorum and be able to conduct the meeting. Members who have lost their voting rights for some reason would not have their votes counted toward the total votes, nor would their votes be counted towards the quorum. Without having 100 members, who are entitled to vote, present in person or by absentee ballot, then the members meeting cannot take place because the quorum has not been met.

**Board of Directors Meeting**: The quorum required for a board of directors meeting will most likely be stated in the Bylaws as requiring that the majority of directors constitute a quorum. If there is a nine member board, then the majority number of five directors would be required to be present in order to have a quorum and conduct the meeting.

There will normally be an odd number of directors required for the board. In the event of a resignation, there may be a couple of meetings where a former nine member board will be an eight member board until a replacement member is appointed. Since a simple majority, in this case, would be a fraction, (4.1) and directors can't be divided into fractions, it would still require five directors to be present in order to have a quorum.

A director may be at a distant location, and not able to attend the meeting in person, but may still be allowed to participate in the meeting and be counted for purpose of determining quorum by having a speaker phone system set up so that the remote director can hear everyone and everyone can hear the director.

## *The Absence of a Quorum*

If there are not enough members present to constitute a quorum, there cannot be any business conducted. The meeting may be called to order, and wait a few minutes to see if others will show up so there is a quorum. If a quorum cannot be established, then the meeting must be adjourned due to lack of quorum.

## *Committee Meetings*

If the Bylaws do not specify how many committee members are required to constitute a quorum, then the committee should establish the quorum to be a majority of committee members.

## *Why is a Quorum Necessary?*

The purpose of all of the procedures in Robert's Rules, or other parliamentary systems, is to allow the majority to make the decisions while protecting the right of the minority to be heard. Therefore, the requirement to have a majority of members present in order to conduct business is to protect against decisions being made by an unreasonably small number of members.

**Example:** A Finance Committee has seven members, but they have never established what constitutes a quorum. They should have established that four members (the majority) are required in order to have a quorum to conduct business. But they didn't! On one extraordinary day, at the last minute, five members were unable to attend, leaving two members who could legally have the meeting and conduct business. These two members, constituting a minority, could make decisions that would affect the organization.

94

Of course, at a later meeting, the majority could reverse the decisions made by the minority, but that could cause dissention among the committee members that may negatively affect the atmosphere of future meetings, making it difficult to conduct business in a business-like manner.

# ORDER OF BUSINESS

It is necessary, in order to have an orderly meeting, to establish an agenda for each meeting and stick to that agenda. The president is responsible, after receiving agenda item requests from other directors, to draft the agenda. The New Business items should be in the order of importance, so those items will be assured of being taken up first in the event that the meeting runs overtime and must be adjourned without having taken up all of the items. The items of lesser importance that are missed should be placed in the Unfinished Business category of the agenda for the next meeting so they will be taken up before New Business.

Meetings should run no longer than ninety minutes to two hours. By the end of two hours people will be getting restless, tired, and possibly bored, so tempers can become short. Therefore, the chairman must move the meeting along so that everyone who wishes to speak has the opportunity, but no one should be allowed to ramble on forever.

The sample agenda below has planned times set for the specific items so the chairman can see if the meeting is running long or on schedule.

Times were not placed on each item because some items are inevitably going to take more time than others. Time parameters are only placed on the major categories. Some items will be agreed upon without debate, so they will only take one or two minutes at the most to dispose of. Other items may take 15 or 20 minutes. The time will usually average out as long as the chairman keeps things rolling along in a business meeting like manner. Once an item is voted on and disposed of, the chairman should move on to the next item without hesitation.

In the example below, the meeting is always scheduled for 90 minutes on the agenda template so times don't have to be computed for every meeting. During the meeting, the chairman is able to see at a glance if any item is moving ahead or falling behind schedule. If it's moving ahead, that's good, because it provides extra time if needed for later items. But just because it's ahead of schedule, the pace should not be slowed. Keep going at a steady comfortable pace because extra time may be needed for a later item. If the meeting is getting behind schedule, and if it's possible, the chairman may try to move along a little faster provided it can be done comfortably without members feeling rushed.

# MEETING AGENDA EXAMPLE

Utopia Homeowners Association
Board of Directors Regular Business Meeting
Jumping Jive Clubhouse
February 12, 2015 5:00 P.M.

## *AGENDA*

1.  5:00 **Call Meeting to Order**

2.  **Agenda Approval** of the Regular Business Meeting for February 12, 2015

3.  **Minutes Approval** for the Regular Business Meeting held January 14, 2015

4.  5:05 **Public Forum**

5.  5:20 **Reports**

    i.    President's message
    ii.   Treasurer's report
    iii.  Maintenance report
    iv.   Committee 1 report

6. 5:40 **Unfinished Business**

7. 5:50 **New Business**

   i.    Item name
   ii.   Item name
  iii.   Item name
  iv.   Item name
   v.    Item name

8. 6:30 Adjourn

# Meeting Decorum

Every board meeting and members meeting should have rules of decorum that everyone is familiar with and that the chairman enforces. If the board has adopted Robert's Rules of Order, the chairman should follow the rules of decorum discussed in Robert's Rules of Order > Rules Governing Debate. They are discussed here:

    In Robert's Rules of Order, the word chairman is gender neutral; a female chairman is addressed as Madame Chairman, and a male chairman is addressed as Mr. Chairman.

## *Confine All Remarks to the Merits of the Pending Question*

Any members' remarks must be germane to and have a direct bearing on the question before the board and whether the motion should be adopted.

    Do not interrupt a speaker who has the floor. Every speaker has the right to use his or her time to speak without interruption. The chairman must control the meeting so that interruptions are not allowed.

    All members must refrain from attacking a member or his/her motive. A member can condemn the nature or likely consequences of a proposed issue in strong terms, but he must avoid personalities, and under no circumstances can he attack or question the motives of another member, or call another member a derogatory name. The issue, not the member, is the subject of debate. A member may not call another member a liar or state that the other's statement is false. Instead he can state that there is strong evidence that the member is mistaken.

The moment one member begins to attack another member, the chairman must act immediately and decisively to stop the member, and prevent any recurrence.

## Stick to the Time Restriction

The board should require a time limit, such as 2 minutes, or 3 minutes, depending on the amount of business to be conducted and the overall time allotted for the meeting. Each speaker should be respectful of other members and plan their remarks to fit within the allotted time frame. The chairman does not have the authority to allow extra time. The time limit is set by the board, therefore, only the board may extend the time. If the chairman believes the speaker should have another minute or two, he can say to the board, *"If there is no objection, we will allow the speaker another 2 minutes."* (Then pause.) Next, he can say, *"Hearing no objections, the speaker has another 2 minutes."* If there is an objection, then the speaker either has to stop, or someone on the board can make a motion so that the majority of the board may decide.

## Address all Remarks through the Chair

Generally, all remarks should be addressed through the chair.

## Avoid the Use of Members' Names

The proper way to refer to another person is to say "the member" who spoke last, etc. However, in a small board consisting of neighbors, that requirement may be a bit too impersonal. As long as one's name is not mentioned in a derogatory manner, using the person's name should be ok. It's up to the board how they would like to amend these rules to best fit in with the atmosphere they wish to provide.

## Refrain from Speaking against One's Own Motion

It is permissible to make a motion that the maker does not support and plans to vote against. One reason for making such a motion may be to get it on the table and voted on, knowing it will fail at this time. However, once the motion is made, the maker may not speak against the motion, although he may vote against it when the vote is called for.

## Refrain from Disturbing the Assembly

During a debate, or during remarks being made by the chairman, no member should be permitted to disturb the assembly by whispering, walking across the floor, or being distracting in any other way. The key words are "disturb the assembly." There are times when one needs to get up to go to the bathroom, or whisper something quietly to another person. That's ok as long as it is not distracting to the assembly, and doesn't appear that the person is talking about the speaker instead of listening.

## Active Listening

Every director should learn how to be an active listener. Here are several suggestions:

- Look at the speaker while she is speaking.
- Try to understand what the speaker is communicating.
- Do not be thinking of your response while the speaker has the floor.
- Try to summarize what you believe the speaker is saying in order to show that you are listening closely and want to understand the speaker's position.
- Ask questions to more fully understand what the speaker is trying to communicate.

# CHAPTER 8

# ROBERT'S RULES OF ORDER

## RULES FOR SMALL BOARDS

Robert's Rules Section 1, states that in small boards, most parliamentary rules apply, but certain modifications permitting greater flexibility and informality are commonly allowed.

- Small boards are understood to be no more than twelve members. The relaxed procedure for small boards is described in Robert's Rules Section 49.
- Members may raise a hand instead of standing to obtain the floor, and may remain seated while making motions or speaking.
- Motions need not be seconded.
- There is no limit to the number of times a member can speak to a debatable question.
- Informal discussion of a subject is permitted while no motion is pending.
- When a proposal is perfectly clear to all present, a vote can be taken without a motion having been introduced.
    - The chairman can state: *"if there is no objection, the meeting will be adjourned."* Pause. *"Hearing no objection, the meeting*

*is adjourned."* That is referred to as unanimous consent; if no one objects, it means everyone is in favor.
- The chairman need not rise while putting questions to a vote.
- The chairman may speak in informal discussions and in debate, and may vote on all questions.

# What Does a "Second" Mean?

In Robert's Rules of Order, at least two persons must want to discuss an issue before it can be placed on the table.

The person who makes a motion for a question is the first person who wishes to discuss the question.

The person who "seconds" the motion is the second person who wishes to discuss the question.

If no one seconds the motion, then there is only one person who wishes to discuss the question, therefore, the motion dies and may not proceed to debate.

But what about an issue that has been discussed informally prior to the motion being made? In large boards, informal discussion is not allowed. The reasoning is that if no more than one person wishes to discuss the question, it is not worth bringing to the table. Therefore, no discussion on a question is allowed unless there is a motion and a second.

In small boards, informal discussion is allowed, and since the question will have already been discussed by more than one person, the motion is considered to have been seconded by way of discussion having already taken place. However, a board may have adopted a rule that, after an issue has been informally discussed, it still must have a second prior to entering into formal debate.

### Can I Withdraw my Second?
Prior to the motion being stated by the chair, the seconder may withdraw her second.

After a motion has been stated by the chair, it belongs to the assembly and the majority of the board must agree to allow the withdrawal.

If a motion has been modified, or amended, the seconder can withdraw the second. However, when the seconder withdraws his second to the modified motion, the member who suggested the modification has, in effect, supplied a second.

## Can I Withdraw My Motion?

A request to withdraw a motion can be made any time before voting on the question has begun. The procedure can involve unanimous consent. Rather than ask for a motion, the chairman can state: "Unless there is objection, (the chairman should pause to give time for an objection to be stated) the motion is withdrawn." If there is an objection, the chairman or any other director can make a motion to withdraw the motion. It does not require a second since the maker of the motion to grant permission and the maker of the request surely both favor it.

The meaning of a second, along with when and how it can be withdrawn, and when and how a motion can be withdrawn are basic issues that are raised frequently, and should be memorized by every director.

## Basic Rules for Some Motions

The basic rules for motions may sound complicated but they really aren't. They just require taking a little time to become familiar with. Memorizing all of them is a different story. That takes a lot of time, but is not necessary for the average HOA meeting.

There are cheat sheets that can be referred to at a glance if an unfamiliar motion or issue arises. It will take less time to glance at the sheet to determine the answer than to have directors argue over who is right or wrong on the question, or to have the chairman make an arbitrary decision (which could be the wrong decision).

## Four Basic Types of Motions:

1.  Main Motions:

The main motion is for the purpose of introducing business to the board for deliberation. A main motion has the lowest level of precedence so it cannot be made if another motion is on the floor. Subsidiary and privileged motions have precedence over main motions.

2. Subsidiary Motions:
Subsidiary motions change how a main motion is handled; they must be voted and disposed of before proceeding with the main motion.

3. Privileged Motions:
Privileged motions bring up urgent matters that are unrelated to the pending business.

4. Incidental Motions:
Incidental motions provide a method to question procedures; they must be voted and disposed of before proceeding with the main motion.

## Six Steps for a Motion

The board chairman should be familiar with basic parliamentary rules so he or she can have control over the meeting. There are six steps in proceeding with a motion and every director should be familiar with them.

Many directors basically know how to make a motion but they don't know the steps involved in handling the motions. Consequently, boards at times will get bogged down in argument because the language of the motion is not clear, or someone makes a type of motion that is not proper and the chairman is forced to make a decision to settle the argument. If the chairman isn't familiar with the rules, that decision may not be the correct one. If the six steps are understood and followed, many arguments over procedure should be prevented.

**Step 1: A Director makes a motion.**
The director should first be recognized by the chair before making the motion. The director would then use the words, "I move..." and continue with the motion: "I move that all board members are to receive 100%

increases in pay effectively immediately." She should not explain why the motion is being made at this time.

**Step 2: The motion is seconded.**
Another director says, "I second." One does not need to be recognized by the chair to make the second. Please note that the seconder does not have to be in favor of the motion. He can be opposed to it. Making the second is just saying that he believes the motion should be discussed.

**Step 3: The chairman states the motion.**
This is an important step to understand because it is a pivotal point in the motion procedure. After the motion is seconded, the chairman is to repeat the motion exactly as it is to be debated by saying, "*it is moved and seconded that all board members are to receive 100% increases in pay effectively immediately.*" The language of the motion must not be ambiguous. If it is not stated exactly, then later on there can be confusion as to what is being voted on, or even worse, there could be later confusion as to what the board approved.

After the chairman states the motion, the question belongs to the board, and the rules for amending a motion, withdrawing a motion, or withdrawing a second must be followed.

Prior to the chairman stating the motion, the maker can withdraw or amend the motion, or can accept a request to amend the motion, and the seconder can withdraw the second.

**Step 4: The motion is debated.**
The maker of the motion has the right to speak first, and the right to speak last. If the director wishes to speak first, this is his opportunity if he wishes to explain the reasons for the motion along with any background.

During debate, it is good practice to alternate between those who are opposed and those who are in favor of the motion. The maker of the motion is not allowed to speak in opposition to his own motion. He is permitted to vote against his motion, but may not speak against it.

**Step 5: The chairman puts the question to a vote.**
When the chairman senses that the debate is essentially over, she may ask the directors, "Are we ready for the question," or more informally, "Are we ready to vote?" At this time, the chairman must repeat the motion again. While debating, it's possible for directors to forget the exact language of the motion, and there may be some confusion; that is the reason the chairman must repeat the motion again at this time. The chairman may say, "The question is that 'all board members are to receive 100% increases in pay effectively immediately.' All in favor raise hands. All opposed raise hands."

**Step 6: The chairman announces the results of the vote.**
The chairman then says, "The ayes have it and the motion is approved." Or, "the No's have it and the motion has failed."

You may have noted that the motion is repeated three times during these six steps, and each time for a specific reason. Therefore, it is important for the chairman to follow those six steps in order to avoid any chance of confusion.

# MOTIONS

List of the 13 Motions in Order of Precedence:

1. Fix the Time to Which to Adjourn
2. Adjourn
3. Take a Recess
4. Raise a Question of Privilege
5. Call for the Orders of the Day
6. Lay on the Table
7. Previous Question
8. Limit or Extend Limits of Debate
9. Postpone to a Certain Time
10. Commit or Refer
11. Amend

12. Postpone Indefinitely
13. Main Motion

The Main Motion has the lowest precedence. Any higher motion can be applied to a main motion, and must be resolved prior to returning to the main motion.

When any motion in the list is pending, the motions above it are in order; those below it are not in order.

A main motion may only be made when there is no other motion pending.

## *Meaning of each motion:*

**Fix the Time to Which to Adjourn.**
This schedules the date and time of the adjourned meeting if no other meeting is scheduled. The word "to" in Fix the Time to Which to Adjourn sometimes causes confusion. It may be easier to understand this if you think in terms of adjourning this meeting until a future date. This meeting must be adjourned without completing all of the business. There are no further meetings scheduled. Therefore, there needs to be a date and time scheduled to complete the business. Consequently, the assembly schedules a future meeting date; that date is the "time to which to adjourn".

- Cannot interrupt a speaker
- Must be seconded
- Not debatable
- Amendable
- Majority vote required

**Adjourn.**
Closes the meeting

- Cannot interrupt a speaker
- Must be seconded
- Not debatable

- Amendable
- Majority vote required

**Take a Recess.**
Establishes a brief break

- Cannot interrupt a speaker
- Must be seconded
- Not debatable
- Amendable
- Majority vote required

**Raise a Question of Privilege**
This is an urgent question regarding rights such as room too hot or cold, etc.

- May interrupt a speaker
- No second needed
- Not debatable
- Not amendable
- Ruled by chair

**Call for the Orders of the Day.**
Requires that the chairman follow the agenda

- May interrupt a speaker
- No second needed
- Not debatable
- Not amendable
- Must follow agenda if only one member requests

**Lay on the Table.**
Puts motion aside until later in same meeting, in order to dispose of more urgent business. (This motion is commonly misused. It is erroneously used

when the most appropriate motion would be to Postpone to a Certain Time, or Postpone Indefinitely.)

- May not interrupt a speaker
- Second required
- Not debatable
- Not amendable
- Majority vote required

**Previous Question.**
Ends debate and moves directly to the vote.

- May not interrupt a speaker
- Second required
- Not debatable
- Not amendable
- Two thirds majority required

**Limit or Extend Limits of Debate.**
Changes debate limits

- May not interrupt a speaker
- Second required
- Not debatable
- Amendable
- Two thirds majority required

**Postpone to a Certain Time.**
Puts off motion to a specific time or date

- May not interrupt a speaker
- Second required
- Debatable
- Amendable

- Majority vote required

**Commit or Refer.**
Refers the motion to a committee

- May not interrupt a speaker
- Second required
- Debatable
- Amendable
- Majority vote required

**Amend.**
Proposes a change to a main motion (See details on amendments in next section.)

- May not interrupt a speaker
- Second required
- Debatable
- Amendable
- Majority vote required
- Only two amendments at one time
- Second amendment must be resolved before returning to the first amendment.

**Postpone Indefinitely.**
Kills the motion

- May not interrupt a speaker
- Second required
- Debatable
- Not amendable
- Majority vote required

**Main Motion.**
Brings business before the assembly

- May not interrupt a speaker
- Second required
- Debatable
- Amendable

## How to Amend a Motion

Prior to considering any amendment to a motion, the motion must be carefully stated so that everyone knows the exact wording. Too often, someone discusses an idea for a motion and when the Chairman asks for a motion, someone yells out, "I move what he said!" Well, what did he say? Really now, that is not a motion, and the Chairman should never accept that.

When that happens, the Chairman should ask for someone to help word the motion, and the Chairman can also suggest wording for the motion. The Chairman should write the motion down because she has to state the motion three times during the debate process, and the wording must be precise.

To amend is a subsidiary motion to amend a motion, to modify the wording, and within certain limits, to change the meaning before the pending main motion is voted on. The motion to amend is one of the most used of the subsidiary motions and the full procedure is not generally well understood by most.

When a board takes an action, it is simply adopting a statement that directs a certain action to be carried out, or expresses a certain view. The precise wording of the statement may be crucial if it deals with a complex matter or a controversial issue.

Adoption of an amendment to a motion does not adopt the pending main motion. The motion remains pending as amended and must be voted on in its amended form.

An amendment must always be germane, that is, closely related to the subject of the motion to be amended. No new subject can be introduced under the guise of being an amendment.

## Friendly Amendment

The term friendly amendment describes an amendment offered by someone who is in favor of the purpose of the main motion, and believes that the amendment will improve the effect of the motion, or increase the chance of the motion's adoption. The maker of the motion can accept or not accept the friendly amendment; however, the amendment must still be opened to debate and voted on under the same general amendment rules.

### Three Amendment Processes

There are three processes of amendment; the third is an indivisible combination of the first two ways to amend a motion that is amendable:

1. **First process**: to insert, or to add.
   a. To insert words, or if they are placed at the end of the sentence, to add words.
   b. To insert a paragraph, or if it is placed at the end, to add a paragraph.

2. **Second process**: to strike out.
   a. To strike out words.
   b. To strike out a paragraph.

3. **Third process**: an indivisible combination of processes (1) and (2) having the following forms:
   a. To strike out and insert (which applies to words).
   b. To substitute; that is, in effect, to strike out a paragraph, or the entire text of a motion and insert another in its place.

Before a first amendment, which is termed the primary amendment, is voted on, it can be amended by a secondary amendment (a motion to amend the amendment). The secondary amendment can only amend the struck out, inserted, or added words or paragraphs. In other words, a secondary amendment is only amending the primary amendment; it cannot amend the pending motion.

There can only be two amendments at one time, the primary and secondary amendments. There cannot be three amendments pending at one time. If the secondary amendment is approved, then another secondary amendment may be made to amend the primary amendment.

**Improper Amendments:**

1. One that is not germane to the question to be amended.

2. One that merely makes the adoption of the amended question equivalent to a rejection of the original motion. Here is an example: The motion is, "The board shall authorize the manager to purchase a new desk." An amendment to insert the word "not" after the word "shall" is out of order because an affirmative vote on not giving the authorization is identical to a negative vote on giving the same authorization.

3. One that would cause the question as amended to be out of order.

4. One that proposes to change one of the forms of amendments listed in Roberts Rules into another form.

5. One that would have the effect of converting one parliamentary motion into another. A motion to postpone the question until 2 pm cannot be amended by striking "until 2 pm" and inserting "indefinitely," since this would convert it into a different kind of motion. There are two different postpone motions:
   a. Postpone to a certain time
   b. Postpone indefinitely

6. One that strikes the word Resolved or other enacting words.

## *Motions that Cannot be Amended:*

- Adjourn
- Question of Privilege
- Orders of the Day
- Lay on the Table
- Take from the Table
- Previous Question
- Point of Order
- Appeal
- Parliamentary Inquiry
- Suspend the Rules
- Reconsider.

## *Sample Motion and Amendments*

Let's amend this sample motion:

**Member A**: I move that the association buy an oak desk for the secretary.

**Member B**: I second.

**Chairman**: The question is that "the association buy an oak desk for the secretary." Is there any discussion?

**Member C**: I move to amend the motion by inserting the word "new" before the word "oak."

**Member B**: I second.

**Chairman:** The question is on a primary amendment to the motion, to amend the motion by inserting the word "new" before the word "oak." Is there any discussion?

**Member D**: I move to amend the amendment by substituting the word "oak" with the word "maple."

**Chairman:** The motion is out of order. A secondary amendment is only to amend the primary amendment. We can vote to approve the primary amendment now, and then make your motion as a primary motion to the pending main motion. Are you ready for the question on the primary amendment?

**Chairman**: The question is on the amendment to the main motion to insert the word "new" before the word "oak."

**Calls for Votes:** The "ayes" have it, the motion to insert the word "new" before the word "oak" is approved.

**Member D**: I move to amend the main motion to substitute the word "oak" with the word "maple."

**Member Y:** I second.

**Chairman**: The question is on the primary amendment to substitute the word "oak" with the word "maple."

**Call for Votes**: The "ayes" have it. The motion to amend the pending motion to substitute the word "oak" with the word "maple" is approved.

**Chairman**: The main motion as amended is, "That we buy a new maple desk." Is there any discussion?

**Call for Votes:** The ayes have it; the motion as amended, "That we buy a new maple desk for the secretary" is approved.

With a little study to become familiar with the three basic processes of amendments, you'll know that other forms of amendment are not in order. With a little practice, the processes can be mastered fairly easily. Utilizing these three processes in meetings will prevent confusion among members so that meetings should flow more smoothly with fewer misunderstandings.

## *Minutes*

The secretary has the responsibility and duty of taking the minutes of a board meeting. In associations where there is a management company, the property manager may be delegated the duty of physically taking the minutes; however, the responsibility for the minutes cannot be delegated. The secretary is still responsible to see that the minutes are recorded accurately, and maintained in accordance with the records retention law of the state.

Until the minutes of one meeting are approved by the board at the next meeting, they are unofficial and should not be distributed. That's because the minutes could contain some transcription errors. After the board reviews and approves the minutes, they become the official record of that meeting and may be distributed to the membership, or made available on the association web site.

Robert's Rules of Order Section 48 makes the following statements:

> *"…the minutes should contain mainly a record of what was <u>done</u> at the meeting, not what was <u>said</u> by the members. The minutes should never reflect the secretary's opinion, favorable or otherwise, on anything said or done…."*

Some would like to see more information in the minutes, such as what the directors said, but that is not what the minutes are for. The minutes are to maintain a record of the <u>actions</u> taken by the board. Therefore, it is imperative that the minutes be accurate. In order to be accurate, the wording of any motion must be recorded exactly as it was stated. If a motion is paraphrased, then later on there can be a misunderstanding of exactly what action was taken by the board.

If the secretary, or the person to whom the duty of taking the minutes was delegated, elects to record some of the conversation in order to appease those wishing to have more information, then the information recorded becomes subjective. The person recording the minutes will make a subjective decision on what parts of the debate to record, and although it was done innocently, the information recorded could be misleading, misunderstood, or out of context.

Therefore, it is a best practice to follow Robert's Rules of Order, and the advice that many HOA attorneys provide, which is to record what was done — not what was said.

## Association Records Retention

If an Association is managed by a professional manager, or a professional management company, they will have a record retention schedule that shows how long each type of record should be kept. However, that does not relieve the secretary, and the board, from the responsibility to see that the records are being kept in accordance with the law.

In addition to what the record retention law requires, HOA experts recommend some records to be kept longer. Below are examples of the time some records are recommended to be kept:

- Minutes of board meetings should be kept permanently;
- All communications with members are required to be kept for three years;
- According to an Arizona HOA attorney, that would include emails, letters, and communications regarding CC&R violations such as
  - Notices of Non-compliance;
  - Notices of Violations;
  - Notice of Hearing;
  - Notice of Fines;
  - Any other written communication with the members.
- All financial documents should be kept for 7 years because the IRS could require those records for an audit.

Below is the complete Arizona records retention law:

## 10 -11601. Corporate records

A. A corporation shall keep as permanent records minutes of all meetings of its members and board of directors, a record of all actions taken by the members or board of directors without a meeting and a record of all actions taken by a committee of the board of directors on behalf of the corporation.

B. A corporation shall maintain appropriate accounting records.

C. A corporation or its agent shall maintain a record of its members in a form that permits preparation of a list of the names and addresses of all members and in alphabetical order by class of membership showing the number of votes each member is entitled to cast and the class of memberships held by each member.

D. A corporation shall maintain its records in written form or in another form capable of conversion into written form within a reasonable time.

E. A corporation shall keep a copy of all of the following records at its principal office, at its known place of business or at the office of its statutory agent:
1. Its articles or restated articles of incorporation and all amendments to them currently in effect.
2. Its bylaws or restated bylaws and all amendments to them currently in effect.
3. Resolutions adopted by its board of directors relating to the characteristics, qualifications, rights, limitations and obligations of members or any class or category of members.
4. The minutes of all members' meetings and records of all actions taken by members without a meeting for the past three years.

5. All written communications to members generally within the past three years, including the financial statements furnished for the past three years under section 10-11620.
6. A list of the names and business addresses of its current directors and officers.
7. Its most recent annual report delivered to the commission under section 10-11622.
8. An agreement among members under section 10-3732.

F. Notwithstanding this chapter, a condominium association shall comply with title 33, chapter 9 and a planned community association shall comply with title 33, chapter 16 to the extent that this chapter is inconsistent with title 33, chapters 9 and 16.

# FINANCES

## BUDGET

A large association with an in-house manager or a community management company usually has the budget for the next year prepared for the board to approve. Prior to the budget being prepared, the preparer should have input from the entire board. The input will be on what expense items the board believes should be increased or decreased, and if the board feels there is a need for an increase in dues.

The preparer should examine every line item to see if the expense can be reduced. Good directors should examine all expenses in order to keep the association expenses at the lowest level possible. There will usually be some padding in certain types of variable expenses because their exact number will be unknown, and it's better to have more budgeted than necessary than not enough, but the padding should be kept to a minimum. There can be a tendency to overspend if directors rely on the padding of the variable expenses to

cover over-spending on other expenses. View the budget as if you are preparing a budget for your own money in your personally owned business.

The budget sheet will have expenses shown for each expense item for each of the twelve months. Some expenses items may be paid quarterly and some may be paid on an annual basis. The budget sheet will show the month the expense is scheduled to be paid.

For each month, there will be three columns with these titles:

### Budgeted
This is the amount of money budgeted to be spent for an expense during the month.

### Actual
This is the amount of money that was actually spent.

### Variance
This will show whether the money spent was over or under budget.

The reserve specialist will determine how much money the association should budget to contribute to the reserve funds account each month in order to maintain the reserve fund at the desired funding percentage.

The association may also wish to save money for unknown capital improvements that members may wish to complete in the future. The reserve fund monies are earmarked for the major repair and replacement of specific existing assets. They can, but shouldn't be, used for new projects that are considered to be capital improvements; therefore, the board should add a new line item to contribute money monthly to the capital improvement account for new projects. If a board does use money from the reserves to fund a capital improvement, plans should be made to replace that money in the reserves account.

## SPECIAL ASSESSMENTS

If no community members are coming to the board meetings, the board may be lonely, and in need of company. When that happens, just send out a letter that the board plans to levy a special assessment! You'll have plenty of company at the next meeting—although they will not be happy campers.

If the board has been diligent in performing its duties—collecting assessments, maintaining a low level of delinquencies (there will always be some delinquency), maintaining the community in good condition so that there are no extraordinary repairs caused by neglect, keeping a lid on expenses, getting competitive bids for required work, and contributing the necessary amount of money to fund the reserves properly—then the association should never get to the point of requiring a special assessment.

In many associations, getting approval from the members for a special assessment will be very difficult because homeowners expect the board to do a good job of running the association business, and will be extremely vocal and critical when they learn that an assessment is needed, assuming that it means the board has not done such a good job.

If there are extenuating circumstances where the board is not at fault, then the board may be able to get approval for the assessment, although the members are never happy about spending more.

To get approval for a special assessment, some communities may require a 2/3 affirmative vote of the members voting in person or by absentee ballot. The quorum may require that 60% of the members be present in person or by absentee ballot. Using an example for a community with 1,200 homes, 720 owners would need to vote either by absentee ballot or in person, in order to constitute a quorum, and 480 of the votes would have to be in the affirmative in order for the special assessment to pass.

If the board presents a solid enough case for needing the special assessment, and can ensure that there will not be a need for another one, then it may be possible to sell, but special assessments are highly unpopular with homeowners, therefore, any special assessment will be a tough sell.

# Five Year Plan

Every association should have a road map of where they are going, how they plan to get there, and what it will look like when they arrive. It takes planning to develop a good road map, but having that map will most certainly help the journey go more smoothly. Proper planning and enhancements to the road map will help prevent many fires from cropping up, so the board can devote more time to the job of governing the association rather than putting out fires.

Part of the planning process is to define, schedule, and budget for preventative maintenance. When preventative maintenance is performed as scheduled, it eliminates much of the emergency work of having to deal with unanticipated equipment failure.

It's similar to having your car inspected at the factory recommended intervals which includes rotating tires, checking air pressure, changing oil, filters, and the inspection of other parts. When the preventative maintenance is performed as required, the car should run for years without having any unanticipated failures. Of course, that isn't absolutely correct because some parts will fail due to factory defects, road damage, or other unpreventable reasons, but those types of failures will be minimal.

## Communication

Part of the planning process in this new digital age should include researching more effective means of communicating to the members in order to better keep them informed. As communities mature, there will be a changing need for amenities; therefore, the board should continuously look at improving the existing amenities and exploring new ones to satisfy the community's ever-changing needs.

Here's one example of planning ahead: More and more electric cars are being built every day and those cars need to be charged. Your community may only have one or two electric car owners now, but in five years it may have 25% or more. So, isn't it reasonable for the board to be talking with residents now to see if there is sufficient interest in obtaining a charging station for the community?

If the community response is favorable, then the board can assign a committee to determine the best location for the station, and obtain estimates from several companies who supply, install, and service charging equipment. At this early stage, there is no rush; the committee can take their time and do a lot of research to present to the board for consideration. If the committee recommends charging stations, and the board elects to approve them, they could instruct the treasurer to include a capital improvement line item in the budget for money to be saved for the purchase of the charging station(s) in three years.

That planning method is much more efficient than waiting for three years when there are many electric car owners in the community making requests for a charging station. That places the board under pressure to make a decision quickly. Since there has been no planning, the association probably won't have the funds available, and certainly not budgeted, so they may have to turn down the request, or begin the study at that late date.

During the initial planning phase, the committee may determine that it would not be cost effective for the association to provide charging stations. Consequently, if residents request charging stations in the future, the board will have already made the determination that it is not in the best interest of the community to supply charging stations.

## *Brainstorm*
A five year plan will take some time to develop and should have input from all members of the board and the members of the community. To begin the process, there should be a special meeting scheduled where the board, and others present, can brainstorm about what the community should be five years from now. The plan can have stepping stones; that is, what will be done in year one, two, etc., in order to reach the five year goal.

## *Mission Statement*
Before the brainstorming session(s) begin, the board should develop a mission statement which defines the overall purpose of the association. A mission statement is broad, so in order to fulfill that mission, the board will need to define goals and the steps necessary to achieve those goals.

## *Assessment*
Prior to working on the goals and objectives, the board should make an assessment of the positives and negatives of the association, explore any

opportunities, and identify any potential problems that may face the association in the future.

That will help the board determine how successful it should be in reaching the goals and fulfilling the mission statement.

## Financials

In order to begin a five year plan the board needs to know the current financial condition.

- Review the balance sheet.
- Study the income and expense statement.
- Check the budget to make sure sufficient money is being budgeted for reserves.
- Review the reserve study to determine how well the reserves are funded.

## Volunteers

Developing a five year plan, implementing it and monitoring the progress over the years to keep it on track while making any necessary modifications, will take a number of volunteers with certain knowledge and experience. The board needs to determine what volunteers are needed, and then find out who is available and willing to assist on committees to develop and oversee the project.

This is where communication with the members is vital. Once the board determines what knowledge is necessary for each type of committee, they should reach out for volunteers through the association's communication channels. Of course, if the board has been proactive, it will have already reached out for people to volunteer, and will have a list of names along with their areas of expertise, that the board can refer to when qualified volunteers are needed.

## List of Suggestions

After the financial condition of the association and the reserve funding situation is studied, you're ready to have a special meeting to develop ideas for what the community needs over the next five years. Make a list of every suggestion offered during the meeting, and then analyze that list to see what makes sense for the community and what doesn't. Remember, as fiduciaries for the association, directors must make decisions based on what is best for the community as a whole, not what is best for a few members who may be the "squeaky wheels."

Begin placing the reasonable suggestions onto a list. Later you can ballpark the cost of each individual suggestion to see if it would be financially feasible to consider. A suggested item may not be possible now, but may be workable if it's budgeted for a future date; the association can begin saving for that item at this time. The items that can be completed with the current available funds should be placed at the top of the list in order of priority.

## Maintenance Committee
A physical study of all of the association assets should be made by a committee of members who have knowledge in construction and building maintenance. This experienced committee can identify items that require regular preventative maintenance. They will develop a schedule that includes regular inspections and maintenance. Just as with the automobile example, this type of preventative maintenance procedure should save money by avoiding unexpected failures of equipment due to neglected maintenance.

## Work the Plan
Once the plan is developed, the plan progress should be discussed and reviewed at every board meeting to ensure that the plan stays on schedule. Modifications to the plan may be necessary from time to time due to changing financial status, or changing community needs. By carefully monitoring the plan, any necessary modifications will be recognized early, and the necessary changes can be made.

## Template
The next section may be used by a board as a template for a starting point in guiding your association through the development of a five year plan. It begins with the Mission Statement. The template below uses a golf

community as the example. The number of years can actually vary; it can be any number of years the board feels they can reasonably project into the future.

The template is only a starting point. The entire template may be modified to suit the needs of your association.

## Mission Statement

To increase the desirability of the community, maintain a high quality of life for community homeowners and families, and to maximize the value of their property. This will be accomplished through:

- Efficient and effective administration of the association's assets
- Providing a comfortable living environment of which members are proud
- Protecting and preserving the beauty of the golf course setting
- Delivering thoughtful, friendly and consistent service to the members
- Establishing, maintaining, and enforcing reasonable and currently acceptable standards in order to sustain the beauty, character and integrity of the community

### Positives

- Desirable golf location
- Beautiful clubhouse and many amenities
- Excellent financial condition
- Sound reserve fund
- Name recognition in the area
- Golf associated revenue
- Low association dues

## Negatives

- Small number of regular volunteers
- No oversight committees
- Lack of long-term goals
- Exposure to legal risks
- Reliance on golfing popularity for income

## Opportunities

- Members are probably willing to help if requested
- Policies can be modeled after industry best practices
- Five year plan can be developed to improve assets and conserve funds

## Potential Problems

- Challenges to keep fairways green with the existing budget
- Keeping competitive rates and still making a profit
- Limited number of qualified and interested candidates for board of director seats
- Economy downturn could reduce golf-related income

## Major Focus — Communications

Goal: To more effectively communicate with members

### Strategies to Achieve Goal

- Encourage members to attend board meetings
- Remind members of the board's policy making and strategic planning function
- Discuss plans at board meetings
- Communicate regularly about community functions and events

- Make timely special announcements
- Periodic president's community update letter
- Provide an annual summary of accomplishments

## *Major Focus — Resources*
Goal: Manage and Improve Community Assets

**Strategies to Achieve Goal**

- Have oversight committee conduct routine "completed work" and annual or semi-annual inspection of assets.
- Establish a preventative maintenance program.
- Conduct a reserve study every 2-3 years ad required.
- Establish standard policies and procedures for the board and for committees to ensure that best practices are established.
- Consider educating committee members to become future board members.
- Recognize committee members at annual meetings.

## *Major Focus — Rules and Regulations*
Goal: Ensure that Rules and Guidelines comply with the law and CC&R's

**Strategies to Achieve Goal**

- Place "Update for New Laws" in the annual calendar of required events.
- Review rules at least once a year to see that they are modified to keep up with changing times, and that any new rule does not conflict with the CC&R's.
- Enforce the rules evenly.
- Review compliance letters annually to see if they can be improved in any manner so as to be more effective.

# CHAPTER 10

# MAINTENANCE

## RESERVE STUDY

A reserve study is a long-range planning tool for the major repair and replacement of a community association's physical assets as they reach the end of their useful life.

The association must budget for the eventual large expenditure of funds to provide for a major repair, upgrade, or complete replacement of those assets. That means conducting an inventory and making a list of every asset owned by the association, then determining the life expectancy of each asset.

Let's take a building roof as an example. Assume a building's tile roof has a life expectancy of 40 years and the anticipated cost to replace it in 40 years, adjusted for inflation, is $30,000. Divide $30,000 by 40 years to arrive at the amount of money that must be contributed to the roof reserve fund line item each year in order to have the funds available to replace the roof in 40 years. In this example, $750 must be contributed each year. That process must be repeated for each asset.

The "best practice" way to accomplish this is to hire a Reserve Study Specialist to do the inventory with an association representative who is familiar with every asset of the association, so that no items are overlooked.

The specialist will then determine a "useful life" and "cost to replace" for each item. If the useful life of the roof is 40 years, and the roof is already 15 years old, then the line item will show the remaining life of 25 years for that item. The reserve study should be updated at least every 2-5 years.

Providing the reserve study and keeping it updated demonstrates that the board is acting in accordance with its fiduciary duty, and reduces the individual directors' exposure to risk of personal liability from any financial mismanagement claims.

Although at present, Arizona has no law dealing with reserve funds, the funds for operating expenses and reserve replacement expenses should be kept in separate bank accounts and not be commingled.

I was informed by HOA attorney Jonathan Olcott that a board may use reserve funds for some capital improvements, but they should be prudent and repay the funds so the reserve account doesn't get underfunded.

The reserve fund should be funded at a level that will provide the association with the necessary funds to repair or replace existing assets as needed. The association should have a regular set amount that is budgeted to go into the reserve account each month. This regular contribution method will ensure that the expenses are evenly shared by each owner over the years.

When the board keeps the reserve fund properly funded, it ensures that today's owners who are enjoying the use of the amenities are paying their fair share. If the reserves are underfunded, the future owners will have to make up for the short-fall of the current and previous owners. Consequently, if the board allows reserve funds to become underfunded, they may be exposing themselves to potential personal liability.

## *There are three funding levels:*

1. **Full 100% funding**
   a. As the asset ages, the fund grows in proportion so that it is fully funded at the estimated end of the useful life.

2. **Baseline funding**
   a. This allows the reserves to get to, but not below, zero. In this method, there are funds available but there is a high risk of a special assessment or not being able to repair or replace an asset.

3. **Threshold funding**
   a. This is any percentage of full funding between zero and 100% that an association chooses to maintain.
   b. An association may feel that there are many assets that may never need replacing because of periodic operational type maintenance and repair, therefore, they don't need to be at 100% funded, so they could choose to be at 80% funded, for example, which is in the low risk category of requiring a special assessment.

## *Risk of Special Assessment*

- 70-130% Funded — Low
- 30-70% Funded — Medium
- 0-30% Funded — High

# CHAPTER 11

# ROGUE DIRECTORS AND BOARDS

## THE "ROGUE" DIRECTOR

A director who is accused by the rest of the board of being a "rogue" director should be dealt with diplomatically and systematically. That's because the director may have not been educated in HOA operation and may not understand that he may be doing something wrong or illegal. In that case, he may not initially accept the accusation of being a rogue. Many times, the behavior of a so-called rogue director may be the result of the association not making an effort to educate its board members on HOA operations and proper meeting decorum.

The board first needs to document the actions of the rogue director, make sure they are absolutely correct in their accusations, and then present the director with the observations in an executive meeting. The accused director must then be afforded an uninterrupted opportunity to respond and explain his/her actions.

This informal discussion should be conducted in a friendly atmosphere where it's explained matter of factly that the concern of the board is that the directors' action(s) could potentially place the association at risk for legal action against the association; those potential legal risks should be spelled out so that the accused director can fully understand.

If an agreement on future director actions is not reached with the director, and the conduct continues, then it is time to discuss the issue in an open meeting so the community is aware that the board has an issue with a director whom they believe could place the association at legal risk, and that the board is taking an action to cure the problem. The minutes should reflect that a discussion took place and whatever action was taken by the board.

Care must be taken to only discuss the facts surrounding the "issue," what the director has done that is a violation of the law or the governing documents, the proof the board has of the allegations, and how the director's actions may be detrimental to the association. Do not, under any circumstances, verbally attack the director, or say things about him/her personally. Only discuss his actions that are in violation. Stick to the facts for which you have solid proof!

Remember, in Chapter 4 ARS 10-3830 D states in part,

> "...A director is presumed in all cases to have acted, failed to act or otherwise discharged such director's duties in accordance with subsection A...."

> "...The burden is on the party challenging a director's action, failure to act or other discharge of duties to establish by clear and convincing evidence facts rebutting the presumption...."

Following the open board meeting, if the conduct continues, then the board should write a formal letter of complaint and inform the director that if the conduct continues, the board will call a special members meeting and explain to the members that the director's conduct has reached the point of risk to the association that the board is requesting that members begin a process to recall the director.

Prior to the situation reaching this point, it is advisable to seek the advice of the association attorney.

In Arizona, under criminal or fraudulent type conduct, a director may be removed by judicial proceeding in accordance with ARS 10-809. Also, ARS 33-1813 4(e) states:

> *"If a civil action is filed regarding the removal of a board member, the prevailing party in the civil action shall be awarded its reasonable attorney fees and costs."*

By properly and respectfully addressing the issue with the accused director, the issue may be resolved early on. The board should do everything possible to prevent having to escalate, and especially to prevent having to resort to requesting the membership to remove the director.

## The "Rogue" Board

### But what if instead of a rogue director, the board is a "rogue" board?

Search the Internet for rogue boards, and you'll find many articles discussing, "The board from Hell", "The fascist board," "Runaway board," and many other unfavorable labels. But do the directors that make up these boards recognize themselves as being a "rogue" board? Probably not. They're most likely thinking that what they're doing is the right thing, even if it doesn't comply with the governing documents or the law! In fact, many directors on these so-called "rogue" boards are probably not familiar with their governing documents or applicable laws. Consequently, they probably don't know if they're doing things right or wrong.

So, what constitutes a "rogue" board? Here are a few thoughts:

A board:

- that has secret meetings with several board members in order to control an issue;
- that allows the president or a couple of directors to make decisions without full board approval;
- that discusses issues in closed executive session that should only be discussed in open meetings;
- that will bully association members who disagree with its position;
- that will bully individual directors who disagree with their opinions;
- that will not manage the association employees properly, allowing a manager or management company to run wild;
- that will not enforce the CC&R's evenly; and
- that will not disclose individual conflicts of interest when hiring their relatives, friends, or business associates.

It's very expensive for an individual homeowner to hire an attorney to fight a runaway board because the board has the use of the association attorney who is being paid for by association members.

## Protection for Members

In Arizona, if a homeowner receives a CC&R violation notice, in accordance with ARS 33-1803, the homeowner may petition for an administrative hearing on the matter in the state real estate department pursuant to section 322199.01. The fee for the hearing is currently $500.00, which is steep enough to prevent nuisance complaints, but reasonable enough for a valid complaint against an association. At around $300 per hour for a good attorney who represents homeowners against associations, the $500 fee for the administrative hearing is a good alternative.

Unfortunately, the administrative hearing is only for homeowners filing complaints against associations. The department does not allow hearings in disputes between directors and associations. Consequently, a director who believes he or she is being bullied by a board and association attorney has no alternative but to hire an attorney to fight the board.

## Indemnification

There may be one source of protection for a director who is being bullied by a rogue board. Check your Articles of Incorporation and Bylaws to locate the indemnity section and take that to an HOA attorney who represents homeowners against associations for interpretation. It may provide that a director shall be indemnified if any type of legal action is taken against the director and the allegations cannot be proven. Also, in Arizona, check out ARS 10-3851 and 3852.

It is not the purpose of this book to malign or accuse individual directors or boards of being "rogue".

The purpose of this book is to encourage all HOA directors to become educated in HOA operation, have a working knowledge of the applicable state, federal, and local laws, and the associations' governing documents. It is my belief that boards whose directors are educated in HOA operations and HOA laws will function more efficiently.

# CHAPTER 12

# LEGAL AND FINANCIAL ADVISORS

## THE ROLE OF THE ASSOCIATION ATTORNEY

Board members and homeowners alike should understand the role of the association attorney. Everyone needs to know specifically who the attorney represents, and who he or she does not represent. Here's the skinny on that!

- The board of directors hires the association attorney.
- The attorney is hired to represent the association.
- The attorney does not represent the board of directors.
- The attorney does not represent the manager.
- The attorney does not represent the management company.
- The attorney does not represent individual board members.
- The attorney represents the association.

Although the attorney takes his or her direction from the board, the attorney's undivided loyalty must be to the association, and his or her duty at all times is to act in the best interest of the association—not in the best interest of the board or any individual board member.

There may be times when a board wants an opinion from the attorney who will tell them what they "want" to hear, not what they "need" to hear, even though what they want to hear may be in conflict with the law or the governing documents. This is where the attorney, whose undivided loyalty must be to the association, and whose duty is to keep the association out of legal trouble, must tell the board what they "need" to hear.

Sound confusing? This should make it very clear:

The attorney represents the "association," and no matter what the board wants, the attorney should always provide advice that is most likely to keep the association out of legal trouble.

## Conflicts

The association attorney should not represent any person or entity that may have a conflict of interest with the association. If most of the attorney's business comes from representing homeowners living in HOA's, then the association should not hire that attorney.

A board should not hire an attorney who represents one of the directors in his or her personal business because of the potential, or perceived, conflict of interest. The attorney is required to be 100% loyal to the association, but in that type of conflicted situation, the attorney's loyalty is not undivided.

Directors should closely read and analyze the opinions presented by the attorney, and not blindly accept them. If the opinions have the appearance of possibly creating a conflict that could lead to legal action, or if any opinion actually leads to legal action, the board may have the fiduciary duty to consider interviewing other attorneys and possibly hire a different attorney who is more likely to provide counsel that will keep the association out of legal risk situations.

Attorneys have different methods of operation: Some are prone to conflict, so the opinions they offer boards may create conflict between the board and the association members, or between the board and individual board members. Most conflicts will almost inevitably cost the association a lot of money in attorney fees.

There are other attorneys who are prone to avoid conflicts. They are possessed of a very different personality than the attorney who is prone to conflict. In my opinion, it is more productive, less expensive, and less stressful to hire an attorney who seeks to avoid conflicts.

# ARS 10-3830. General standards of conduct for directors

A director's duties, including duties as a member of a committee, shall be discharged:

- In good faith.
- With the care an ordinarily prudent person in a like position would exercise under similar circumstances.
- In a manner the director reasonably believes to be in the best interests of the corporation.

These duties should be in the back of the mind of every director during every decision he or she is required to make.

Boards should be pro-active, and when they see something happening that appears to be not right, or may possibly be in violation of the governing documents or the applicable laws, they have a duty to the association to investigate, and correct the situation if it isn't as it should be. Understanding the Business Judgment Rule (*which is discussed in the next section*) as it applies to ARS 10-3830 will go a long way toward keeping both the association and individual board members out of legal trouble.

## Attorneys

Vendors generally see homeowner associations as "deep pockets" governed by a board of directors consisting of volunteers who are probably not educated in HOA operation, and managed by managers or management companies who are not dealing with their own personal money. This can lead to many vendors trying to make as much money as possible from the associations. Attorneys are no different than other vendors. The only difference is their skill set, or line of work. But in the subject of wanting to make as much money as possible from associations, it is my personal opinion that many attorneys are the same as other vendors who have the same mindset.

Some attorneys will charge the association for every phone call and every email in $1/10^{th}$ of an hour increments. That is, 6 minute increments. If a phone call lasts one or two minutes, as many phone calls do, the association is billed for six minutes. Those extra one and two minutes billed in $1/10$ of an hour increments can amount to a lot of money over the period of a year.

Large associations will most likely need an attorney's advice and opinion many times during the year, therefore, the association should negotiate a billing method with the attorney that will be more beneficial to the association, and still allow the attorney to make money.

### Flat Rate Attorneys

There are some excellent attorneys who offer flat rate billings.

Several years ago, the sub-association board I serve on contracted with a firm that charges the association $50.00 per month, or $600.00 per year. That fee is paid whether or not we talk to them. However, we have the ability to ask as many questions as we wish each month for that flat rate, in addition to other included services. So, it's possible that we could use one or more hours of their time each month for the small amount of $50.00. But we don't — and that is one way they make their money. They also make money in the delinquency collections process. They have many clients paying them $50.00 per month, and many of those clients may not have any questions for months.

If the association requires an opinion that takes time and research to prepare, there is a separate fee for that, but in most cases, they will quote a flat rate for the opinion. The overall cost to an association for this type of fee arrangement is much less than the other type of fee structure.

Not surprisingly, there are some attorneys who object to a flat rate type of billing and may make derogatory statements about the flat rate attorneys. Nevertheless, the flat rate billing method, with many subscribers paying the flat monthly fee, seems to work well for this firm, and it also works well to keep the legal fees low for associations.

That being said, we must remember that the most important consideration, above the cost savings, is the knowledge, experience, and credibility of individual attorneys and the firm. We ask a lot of questions, and our association has found all of the answers to be in compliance with what we understand the laws to be—and their responses are timely.

Equally important as an attorney firm's experience and knowledge is how they operate when it comes to conflict. Do their opinions appear prone to conflict, which may create more stress and expense for the association, or do they promote peaceful methods of dealing with potential adversaries?

# BUSINESS JUDGMENT RULE

The Business Judgment Rule courts apply in cases where HOA directors are charged with violating their care of duty to the association, comes from ARS 10-3830 Section A:

> "A director's duties, including duties as a member of a committee, shall be discharged:
> 1. In good faith.
> 2. With the care an ordinarily prudent person in a like position would exercise under similar circumstances.
> 3. In a manner the director reasonably believes to be in the best interests of the corporation."

The purpose of the Business Judgment Rule is to protect directors from personal liability in the event a board makes an honest mistake. As long as the Business Judgment Rule is followed, the courts tend to defer to the association. We live in a highly litigious society today and the Business Judgment Rule enables boards to govern their associations without fear of being sued every time a member disagrees with their decision.

The Business Judgment Rule has been applied in many states to community association decision making. Directors have the power and legal authority to govern the association, while members have the right to hold the directors accountable for the decisions they make on behalf of the association. Sometimes, HOA directors will make honest mistakes, and they need assurance that they are protected when they do so while acting in good faith.

If HOA directors had to worry about liability for every decision they make in good faith, it would be very difficult to conduct the association business because they would continuously have to worry about placing themselves at risk of personal liability.

The Business Judgment Rule discourages courts from second guessing directors' decisions that were made in good faith. It is very difficult for a court to determine whether association directors properly evaluated all necessary information prior to making a decision. Therefore, to impose liability on HOA directors for making a wrong decision when they made that decision in good faith, in the manner in which a reasonable person would make in the same situation, and the decision was made in the best interest of the association, would inhibit their ability to make decisions.

When major decisions are made, it is good practice for a board to document any advice from a committee, attorney, accountant, or other professional advisor(s). It's also important for the directors to be certain that the information they are relying on is warranted, because if directors have knowledge, or should have had knowledge, that the information they wish to rely on is wrong, they are not warranted in relying on that information.

See ARS 10-3830 3.C.

*"A director is not acting in good faith if the director has knowledge concerning the matter in question that makes reliance otherwise permitted by subsection B unwarranted."*

The Business Judgment Rule prevents Monday-morning quarterback judging of decisions made by directors in normal situations, but allows liability for decisions made in bad faith and obviously, not in the best interest of the association.

The Business Judgment Rule can be used by courts as a standard of liability test that places the burden of proof on the plaintiff to show that directors acted in bad faith, not in the best interest of the association, or failed to take a required action. If that burden is not met, the courts may apply the Business Judgment Rule.

Any time an issue arises that could potentially lead to legal action, the board should consult with their attorney to obtain a legal opinion. Do not construe any statement in this book to be legal advice.

# DUTIES HOA BOARDS SHOULD NOT DELEGATE TO A MANAGER

HOA management companies and in-house managers can be a great help to an association's board of directors. But a manager should not be allowed to take over the board's duties or responsibilities. Below are some of the duties a board should never allow a manager to perform.

**A board should never abdicate any duties** to a manager that are shown as a power of the board in the Bylaws or other governing documents. That would include the adoption of any Rule, or amending any Rule in the Rules and Regulations.

The Rules and Regulations are an extension of the CC&R's, which is a contract between the association and the association members. The Rules are meant to explain and clarify certain covenants in the CC&R's but they cannot add to, delete, or change the meaning of a covenant. The CC&R's will probably state that any Rules cannot be in conflict with the CC&R's.

If a board develops a Rule that is in conflict with the CC&R's, and enforces that rule against a member, and it's challenged in court by that member, it's possible that a court may consider that to be a breach of contract. If the board has abdicated their responsibility and the manager adopts or amends a rule with language that is in conflict with the CC&R's, the board is still responsible. A board cannot abdicate their responsibility.

It is certainly permissible for a board to have the manager, or a committee, recommend rule adoptions or amendments, however, the board should always review and provide formal approval for any changes.

**Compliance Rules.** Managers should be required to follow strict rules concerning violations, and should not be allowed to waive late fees or make compromises concerning violations. The compliance rules and procedures are adopted by the board for a reason—to be followed—to minimize the association's exposure to legal risks.

In Arizona, the law for notice to members of violations is found in ARS 33-1803. Compliance letters should be drafted in compliance with that law, along with a set of guidelines for the manager to follow. If the guidelines are followed, the rules will be enforced evenly throughout the association, which makes it difficult for a homeowner to charge a board with selectively enforcing the rules.

**Filing a lien against an association member's home.** Only the board should have the authority to make the decision to have a lien filed on an association members' home, and only after careful review of all the records associated with the delinquency. If the board feels that a lien is the next appropriate action, the board should seek the advice of the association attorney. If the attorney's opinion is that a lien is the best course of action, then the board may direct the attorney to proceed with filing the lien.

**Communication with the association attorney.** The manager should have authorization to contact the association attorney for certain limited day-to-day operational questions so the association can run smoothly. For other types of questions requiring attorney communication, only the board should decide who is to be the contact person.

# The CPA and the Auditor

There are three different types of financial examinations performed by CPA's.

- Compilations
- Reviews
- Audits

A Compilation is the lowest level of examination. It is simply the preparation of financial statements from financial information provided by the association.

The Review adds inquiries of the association and analysis not included in a compilation.

The Audit is the most comprehensive, except for a fraud audit, which should rarely be needed. The audit verifies items with outside parties and tests certain transactions by examining supporting documents.

After completing one of the financial examinations, the CPA will present the association with a draft of the financial statements and a representation letter that must be signed by the association. The letter states that no material facts were withheld, and there are no misrepresentations in the documents provided.

The CPA will advise the association whether IRS Form 1120 or Form 1120-H should be utilized.

Just as it is important to hire an attorney who specializes in HOA law, it is important that the CPA should have knowledge and experience in homeowner association and non-profit corporation tax laws.

The association should search for qualified CPA firms and interview each in order to hire the firm that is best suited for the association's requirements.

CHAPTER 13

# CASE STUDIES

## MCNALLY VS. SUN LAKES HOA

Arizona Court of Appeals
October 13, 2016

To read the full appeal ruling you can google McNally vs. Sun Lakes HOA, or click on this link:

http://law.justia.com/cases/arizona/court-of-appeals-division-one-published/2016/1-ca-cv-15-0744.html.

McNally vs Sun Lakes HOA is an interesting case. It is not a long ruling and it's very educational. In my opinion, it should be a must read for all HOA Directors.

My discussion of this case is based on my layperson understanding of the law and how it was applied in this case. Please do not rely on my layperson discussion or opinion about this case or the laws mentioned as legal advice because I am not an attorney.

McNally was a director on the Sun Lakes Board of Directors. Because she began reading an email in an open meeting that the board had elected to not discuss, the HOA attorney apparently advised the board to exclude McNally from attending any further executive meetings.

Eventually, McNally filed a lawsuit against Sun Lakes HOA, and won the case on appeal.

The appeals court ruled that several laws were violated by excluding McNally from participating in executive session meetings.

The court stated that by passing the motion to exclude McNally from participating in executive session meetings, the board prevented her from performing her duties and responsibilities as a director.

- Participating in executive sessions was critical to McNally performing her duties as a director pursuant to ARS 33-1804 (A)(1)-(5). McNally was not allowed to participate in any of those discussions.
- ARS 10-3822 requires that directors be notified of special meetings two days prior to the meeting unless otherwise provided by the articles of incorporation. Those notification requirements guarantee the participation of all board members in managing the affairs of a corporation.
- The court mentioned Title 10 of the non-profit laws in discussing the removal of a board member. It did not discuss Title 33-1813 which was written specifically for Planned Communities. As I understand, from discussions with several attorneys, Title 33-1813, because it was written especially for Planned Communities, would trump what is in Title 10.

HOA attorney Beth Mulcahy made the following statement in one of her "Cheat Sheet" educational publications titled "Board Member Roles and Responsibilities:"

*"Know where to find the state statutes that govern the association or condominium and have a working knowledge of them..."*

I interpret Ms. Mulcahy's statement to mean that all board members who have the duty and responsibility of governing an HOA must have a working knowledge of the laws that govern non-profit corporations and planned communities. Boards are required to comply with those laws.

Without having knowledge of those laws, how can a board make decisions without having a full time attorney on staff whose job it is to quote the law for each policy or business decision the board must make? This brings up several questions to consider for educational purposes:

- Did the board members have a working knowledge of the laws?
- Did the attorney advise the board that it was legal to exclude McMally from executive sessions, or did he tell them that if they exclude her, it could be challenged in court and the association may lose?
- If the attorney advised them that it was legal, and if they did have a working knowledge of the law, were they warranted in following that advice?

These questions are not to be critical or judgmental about McNally or the Sun Lakes board. They are to get us, as board directors, to do more critical thinking about the laws we are required to have a working knowledge of and comply with, so that we can make more educated decisions when faced with similar circumstances.

Much can be learned from studying court cases and asking questions. There are many cases available online for anyone interested in studying them.

## BAD CC&R AMENDMENTS CASE

Here is one more case that I find interesting because of the way the attorney attempted to change the meaning of the words.

Below is the full case report for this hearing. Below the case will be my comments.

**In the Office of Administrative Hearings**
No. 07F-H067029-BFS
Administrative Law Judge Decision
Nancy Waugaman, Petitioner, vs
Troon Village Master Association, Responder

HEARING: July 30, 2007

APPEARANCES: Nancy Waugaman, Petitioner; Carrie Smith and Jason Smith, attorneys, on behalf of Respondent.

ADMINISTRATIVE LAW JUDGE: Michael K. Carroll
On April 6, 2007, a Petition was filed with the Department of Fire Building and Life Safety alleging eight separate violations of state statutes or community documents by Respondent.

**FINDINGS OF FACT AND CONCLUSIONS OF LAW**

**Findings of Fact:**
(1) Petitioner is a member of Troon Village Master Association (Respondent), a planned community comprised of 1,322 members, which is governed by a Declaration of Covenants, Conditions and Restrictions (Declaration), Articles of Incorporation (Articles) and Bylaws.

(2) On October 16, 2006, Respondent's Board of Directors (Board) scheduled a regular meeting. Prior to the time scheduled for the start of the regular meeting, the Board met in executive session with attorneys representing Respondent to discuss a pending lawsuit against Respondent brought by one of the Association's members.

(3) During that session, and in an attempt to avoid future legal problems suggested by that lawsuit, the Board also discussed Section 11.02 of the Declaration which sets forth the voting requirements to amend the Declaration.

Section 11.02 provides:

After the Change Date, the Declaration may be amended by the **affirmative vote of Owners holding at least eighty percent (80%) of the total voting power** in the Association at a meeting duly called pursuant to the Article and Bylaws for the adoption of the amendment.

(4) Following the discussion in executive session, the Board, upon recommendation of its attorneys, passed a Resolution interpreting Section 11.02 to mean that, rather than requiring an affirmative vote of at least 80% *of the entire membership of the Association* to amend the Declaration, **only an affirmative vote of at least 80% of the members voting, either in person or by absentee ballot,** *at a meeting* to amend the Declaration would be required.

Because Article 3, Section 3.5 of the Bylaws defines the "quorum" necessary to conduct business at an Association meeting to constitute 10% of the total voting membership in the Association, the effect of this resolution was to reduce the number of affirmative votes necessary to change the Declaration from a minimum of 1058 votes to a minimum of 106 votes.[1]

(5) The Board based its authority to interpret Section 11.02 of the Declaration on Article 14, Section 14.01 of the Declaration, which provides

Interpretation of the Covenants. Except for judicial construction, the Association, by its Board, shall have the exclusive right to construe and interpret the provisions of this Declaration. In the absence of any adjudication to the contrary by a court of competent jurisdiction, the Association's construction or interpretation of the provisions of this Declaration shall be final, conclusive and binding as to all persons and property benefited or bound by the provisions of this Declaration.

(6) Subsequent to the passage of that Resolution, the Board scheduled a Special Meeting for the purpose of a vote to amend the Declaration to (a) eliminate "tract" voting by the Association and its sub-Associations,[2] (b)

---

[1] 1058 is 80% of all 1,322 members of the Association; 106 is 80% of 132, or 10% of the members necessary to constitute a quorum at an Association meeting.

[2] The main Association and several sub-Associations, which comprised the total membership, were each allotted blocks of votes based upon tracts of land that existed in the community, but which could not be sold as improved lots due to various zoning and building restrictions. The association and the sub-Associations were each assessed

eliminate fee assessments for the "tracts," and (c) create staggered terms for members of the Board. Under the new interpretation of Article 11, Section 11.02 announced in the Board's Resolution, all of these proposed amendments to the Declaration passed.

(7) Following the passage of the amendments to the Declaration, Petitioner filed a Petition with the Department of Fire Building and Life Safety challenging the legality of the actions taken by the Board to amend the Declaration.

**Conclusions of Law:**

Although the Petition listed eight separate counts alleging various violations of state law and documents governing the Association, those counts essentially raise four issues:

(1) Could the Board pass a Resolution interpreting a provision of the Declaration in executive session?

Petitioner argues that the meeting held in executive session was not properly "noticed" as required by A.R.S.§33-1804(C). Petitioner does not dispute that the general meeting scheduled for October 16, 2006 was properly noticed to the membership of the Association. See Respondent's Exhibit 6. She argues, however, that the failure of that notice to include mention of the executive session that took place immediately prior to the open meeting was a violation of notice requirements in A.R.S. §33-1804(C) and Respondent's Bylaws, Section 4.5.

While, ideally, notice of a regular meeting of the Board would make mention of a planned executive session and the purpose for that session (see, for example, Petitioner's Exhibit KK), there is no specific provision in the documents governing Respondent which requires that such notice be provided, nor does such a requirement exist under A.R.S. Title 33, which governs planned communities. Furthermore, if the subject of the executive session is one for which a closed meeting is authorized under A.R.S. §33-1804A (1)-(4), members of the Association who are not also

---

membership fees based upon the size of each Association's "tract." Votes were also allotted to the main Association and the sub-Associations based upon the size of each Association's "tract."

Board members may be excluded, thus lending little purpose to such a notice. Finally, even if the Board failed to provide notice to the membership regarding a planned meeting in executive session, that failure, in itself, would not invalidate any action taken by the Board at that closed meeting. A.R.S. §33-1804C.

Petitioner also alleges that the Resolution passed by the Board in the executive session was not a proper subject for consideration in an executive session and should have occurred with the notice to and the opportunity for discussion by the entire membership of the Association, as required by A.R.S. §33-1804A. As noted above, however, A.R.S. §33-1804A allows meetings to be conducted by the Board in a closed session if, among other things, it involves "legal advice from an attorney for the board or the association." A.R.S. §33-1804A (1).

Respondent maintains that the purpose of the executive session was to discuss pending litigation with the Association's attorney, and, in connection with that discussion, obtain legal advice as to how to proceed in the future with respect to some of the issues raised by that lawsuit. Part of the legal advice imparted by the Association's attorney was that the Board should consider adopting the Resolution, which would interpret the voting requirements for amending the Declaration in a manner that would reduce the total number of affirmative votes necessary to effect such amendments. See written settlement agreement marked as Petitioner's Exhibit AAA.

It would appear that the proposal to pass a resolution changing the interpretation of a key voting provision in the Declaration could have been severed from the discussion regarding the pending litigation, and that the proposed resolution could have been presented for consideration by the entire membership of the association outside of the executive session. However, the issue is not whether the Board could or even should have acted differently, but rather whether the Board's failure to do so was a violation of A.R.S. §33-1804A.

Given the relationship between the pending litigation and the Board's desire to seek the advice of counsel to avoid such legal entanglements in the future, there has been an insufficient showing by a preponderance of the evidence that the Board was acting outside of the scope of its authority, granted by A.R.S. §33-1804A (1), in discussing and passing the Resolution during the executive session. While statutory exceptions to the open meeting requirement should not be used as a guise by boards to shield important association business from membership scrutiny, in this case there was insufficient evidence to suggest that was the Board's purpose. The discussion with the attorneys regarding how to avoid future problems, which had been identified, to a certain extent, by the pending litigation, was reasonably related to the discussions regarding the pending lawsuit which were clearly the proper subject of a closed board meeting.

Furthermore, even if the Board had chosen to conduct a discussion with the entire membership regarding the passage of the Resolution, it still possessed the exclusive right, under Article 14, Section 14.01, of the Declaration, to accept or reject the recommendations of the membership, and to interpret a provision in the Declaration without securing the membership's approval.

(2) Is there any limitation on the Board's use of the authority granted by Article 14, Section 14.01 to effectively change the manner in which the Declaration can be amended by the Association's membership?

Respondent argued that Article 11, Section 11.02 of the Declaration which sets forth the requirements necessary to amend the Declaration was "at least unclear if not completely ambiguous." Respondent further suggested that the drafters of the Declaration anticipated that some of the language used in the Declaration might be "unclear, inconsistent or plain ambiguous." To avoid the problems inherent in competing interpretations of the Declaration, the drafters included Article 14, Section 14.01 to give the Board the exclusive authority to resolve such disputes. See Respondent's Pre-Hearing Brief, p.5.

Although Respondent appears to concede that the Board's authority under Article 14, Section 14.01 is limited to interpretation of only those provisions of the Declaration for which the intent was not clear,[33] Section 14.01 does not contain explicit limiting language to that affect. It merely

---

[3] Even the Resolution passed by the Board indicated the Board's wish to "interpret certain provisions of the Declaration to clarify any ambiguity." Petitioner's Exhibit 1.

provides that the Board "shall have the exclusive right to construe and interpret the provisions of this Declaration."

Despite the broad language of Section 14.01, however, the limitation that Respondent finds implicit in that section appears justified by a simple dictionary analysis of the terms "construe" and "interpret." "Construe" means "to analyze the grammatical structure of a clause or sentence so as to determine the use and function of each word," and "to explain or interpret the meaning" of a clause or sentence." Similarly, "interpret" is defined a "give the meaning [of something]; to make [something] clear." See Webster's Collegiate Dictionary.

Implicit in such definitions is the concept that whatever is being analyzed, explained or clarified is something that is not self-explanatory or self-evident. To ignore such an implicit limitation on the authority granted in Section 14.01 would be to suggest that none of the provisions in the Declaration have their intended meaning if the Board simply chooses to ascribe a different meaning to them. Such a broad interpretation of Section 14.01 would, in essence, allow the Board to nullify any provision of the Declaration. That was clearly not the intent of the drafters of the Declaration, nor is it a reasonable interpretation of the exceptionally broad authority suggested by the language of Section 14.01.

(3) Was Article 11, Section 11.02 of the Declaration ambiguous or unclear?

The pertinent portion of Section 11.02 provides:

…the Declaration may be amended by the affirmative vote of owners holding at least eighty percent (80%) of the total voting power in the Association at a meeting duly called pursuant to the Articles and Bylaws for the adoption of the amendment.

Petitioner argued that the meaning of Section 11.02 is clear. Respondent argued that Section 11.02 is ambiguous because inclusion of the phrase "at a meeting" suggests that only 80% of the total voting power represented at that meeting would be required to amend a provision of the Declaration. In support of that position, Respondent argued that "The 'total voting power *at a meeting*' is quite different from 'total voting power.'" See Respondent's Pre-Hearing Brief, p.5. At the hearing, Respondent cited

*Aldous v. Intermountain Building and Loan Association of Arizona*, 36 Ariz. 225, 284 P. 353 (1930) for the proposition that "It is a cardinal rule of the construction of contracts that some effect is to be given, if possible, to every part thereof." 284 P. at 355.

Applying the principle cited in *Aldous, supra,* to the specific language of the Declaration, Respondent's interpretation of the pertinent part of Section 11.02 would render the qualifying phrase "in the Association" superfluous. If Respondent's interpretation were correct, the drafters of the Declaration could have simply stated that an amendment could be accomplished "by the affirmative vote of Owners holding at least eighty percent (80%) of the total voting power at a meeting duly called pursuant to the Articles and Bylaws for the adoption of the amendment." There would have been no need for the qualifying language "in the Association" unless the drafters intended that 80% of the *entire membership of the association* must vote affirmatively to effect an amendment of the Declaration.[44]

Respondent argued that, unless Section 11.02 is given the interpretation suggested by the Board's Resolution, it is virtually impossible to change any provision of the Declaration even when necessary to account for changes that may arise due to the passage of time, or changes in law, circumstances, etc. In fact, the former Board president testified at the hearing that there had been four different attempts to amend the Declaration since 2005. However, despite overwhelming community support for those proposed amendments, they were unsuccessful because, prior to the Resolution, Section 11.02 had been interpreted by the Board to require an affirmative vote of 80% of the entire membership in the Association. He explained that, because of the difficulty in getting 80% of *all* the owners to even vote in an election to amend the Declaration, much less getting an 80% *affirmative* vote, changes to the Declaration, even though deemed

---

[4] Although Respondent, through counsel, argued that "total voting power" referred to only those members represented at a meeting called to amend the Declaration, the actual wording of the Board's Resolution interpreted the language of 11.02 "to mean that, to amend the Declaration, Owners holding at least eighty percent (80%) of the votes *that are cast,* in person or by absentee ballot, at a meeting duly called, pursuant to the Articles and Bylaws, must vote to affirm the amendment." Petitioner's Exhibit 1.

advisable and even necessary by the vast majority of the members of the Association, were virtually impossible.

Although testimony at the hearing made for a compelling argument that homeowner associations should be wary of making the ability to amend their governing documents too strenuous, it does not obviate the fact that the existing Declaration represents a contract between the Association and its 1,322 members — a contract upon which each of those individual owners had a right to rely. Furthermore, the Board's "interpretation" of Section 11.02 had the effect of allowing as few as 106 members of the association to make significant changes to the contract governing all 1,322 of its members. That was a dramatic change from the Board's belief, prior to the passage of the Resolution, that an affirmative vote of at least 1,058 members of the Association would have been necessary to amend the contract which governed all the Association's members

Article 11, Section 11.02 of the Declaration was not ambiguous on its face. Its meaning was clear, even to the Board prior to October 16, 2006. It was not a proper subject for interpretation under Article 14, Section 14.01, and the Resolution changing the interpretation of Section 11.02 was an invalid exercise of the Board's authority under the Declaration.

(4) Did Respondent deny Petitioner a copy of the Association's mailing list in a "workable format?"

At the hearing, Petitioner testified that Respondent originally responded to her request for a copy of the Association's mailing list by providing her with the information in a "spreadsheet" format, rather than in a "label" format used by Respondent. Although the information was ultimately provided to Petitioner in a "label" format prior to the hearing, Petitioner nevertheless maintained that Respondent's initial failure to provide the "label" format was a violation of A.R.S. §33-1805.

There is nothing contained in either the documents governing the Association or A.R.S. §33-1805 which requires the Respondent to provide information to members in a specific format. A.R.S. §33-1805A simply provides that "all financial and other records of the association shall be made reasonably available for examination by any member..." That statute also requires an association to provide photocopies of records to members if requested. However, the association may charge a fee of not more than $0.15 per page for photocopies.

## ORDER

Based upon the foregoing,

**IT IS ORDERED** vacating the Board's Resolution of October 16, 2006, by which the Board interpreted the meaning of Article 11, Section 11.02 of the Declaration.

**IT IS FURTHER ORDERED** vacating any amendments to the Declaration, passed after the Board's Resolution of October 16, 2006, and which were based upon the affirmative votes cast by 80% of the members, either in person or by absentee ballot at a meeting called for the purpose of amending the Declaration.

**IT IS FURTHER ORDERED** that Respondent shall reimburse the filing fee paid by Petitioner in the amount of $2,000.00.[55]

Done this day, August 13, 2007.

Michael K. Carroll,          Administrative Law Judge
Department of Fire Building and Life Safety — H/C
Robert Barger
Nancy Waugaman
Carrie H. Smith Esq.
Jason Smith, Esq.
Carpenter, Hazelwood, Delgado & Wood, PLC

*My Comments:*

The CC&R's constitute a contract between the homeowners and the association. When a buyer purchases a home in an HOA, he must sign a document stating he is aware that he has entered into a contract with the HOA. When the buyer agrees to that contract and begins to fulfill his responsibilities in the contract, he has the right to expect that the association will also fulfill its responsibilities.

---

5  [5] Pursuant to A.R.S. §41-2198.04(A) this Order is the final administrative decision and is not subject to a request for rehearing.

The reason there is such a large percentage of members required to amend the declaration is because all of those members agreed to the specific terms; therefore, it is paramount that they should be able to vote to agree or disagree with any amendments because an amendment changes a term that they originally agreed on.

Due to the amount of apathy among homeowners, 80% is an almost unattainable number to expect to achieve in any vote, unless the vote is to reduce the dues by 50%, in which case there may be 100% voter turnout.

Therefore, as a board member, I may feel that a lower percentage vote threshold may be more reasonable to pass an amendment.

However, I must remember that homeowner Jones agreed to the original version of the CC&R's. So, let's consider these three scenarios:

1. Suppose the original version said "dogs are allowed," and the amended version said "dogs not allowed." Homeowner Jones did not agree to "no dogs" when she purchased her home; she had dogs and bought a home in the HOA because dogs were allowed; is the board going to have a fool proof method of grandfathering those members like Jones who purchased their homes under the original version?

2. Homeowner Brown didn't own a dog when he bought his home under the original version, but he bought there knowing that there were dogs in the community, and that he could have a dog, and planned to adopt one in the future. After the amendment, is it right to deny homeowner Brown the right to have a dog because he didn't have one when he purchased the home?

3. After the new version was put in place, homeowner Jenkins bought the house next door to homeowner Jones. Jones has a dog because she was grandfathered. Jenkins wants a dog and is angry that Jones has one and she can't. She believes the board is selectively enforcing the rules and files a lawsuit. Will she win?

In the past, I have thought that to reduce the percentage to a simple majority of 51% approval to amend the CC&R's was reasonable. After giving it much thought, and understanding that this is a contract that is being amended, and realizing that many people who agreed to that contract when they purchased their home may not want the contract amended because it may have a negative effect on them, I realized that my thinking was in error. Today, I believe the CC&R's should require a high percentage of owners to approve a change. However, as of this writing, I don't have a percentage number in mind that I feel would be reasonable.

What is your opinion? What percentage of homeowner approval do you believe should be necessary to amend a covenant in the CC&R's?

# Study Questions

This is the section I know you have all been waiting for; the test section! Well, this isn't a test; don't even think of it as a test. This is a section of study questions. It's meant to get you to thinking. It's meant to help you cement what you've read and learned in the previous sections. When you recall an answer to any of the questions, you've proven to yourself that you have mastered that question. When you go back and review the law or section that deals with a question you're unsure of, you will be learning much more.

Many of the Arizona statutes deal with several issues, and as you read them again to answer one question you'll invariably learn more by reading the entire statute. It isn't intended that you'll go through these questions in one sitting either. It will take some time to go through them all.

When you complete studying this book and reviewing the questions, you will be better informed than probably 98% of all homeowner association directors.

**Let's get to it; answer at least a couple of questions a day and soon you'll be an expert!**

1.  What Title and chapters in the Arizona Statutes governs non-profit corporations?

2. What Title and chapter in the Arizona Statutes governs planned communities?

3. List association governing documents in order of precedence.

4. If there is a conflict between the language of the Bylaws and the Articles of Incorporation, which takes precedence?

5. What is the purpose of the Rules and Regulations?

6. If the CC&R's do not prohibit dogs in the community, can the board create a rule to prohibit dogs?

7. Define the "Business Judgment Rule," and its significance to board members.

8. In making a decision, is a director entitled to rely on opinions of professional advisors, such as legal and financial?

9. A homeowner makes a request for documents; how many days does the association have to make those documents available?

10. Can the association charge the homeowner for the documents?

11. What planned community law allows the homeowner to see the association documents?

12. What planned community law governs association meetings?

13. Are all meetings of the members' association, board of directors, and regularly scheduled committee meetings open to all association members?

14. What are the five items a board "may" discuss in executive sessions?

15. The law says the board "may" discuss those subjects in executive session. What is the best practice?

16. For item 5, in 33-1804, "Discussion of a member's violation appeal," the member demands that his appeal be heard in an open meeting; what does the law say about that?

17. What type of committee does not have to provide notice to the members of its meetings, and do not have to hold them in an open meeting?

18. Who elects the directors to the board of directors, the members or the board?

19. In the event of a director's resignation, who can appoint the director's replacement, and how long can the replacement director serve?

20. Which planned community law discusses the removal of a board member?

21. If at least one but less than a majority of directors are removed, what is the procedure for replacement of the directors?

22. If a director is removed, how soon can that director run for the board again?

23. Is there any time that the board of directors can remove a director from the board?

24. If our Bylaws say that a director is absent for three consecutive meetings can have his or her seat vacated by the board, does that mean the board can remove that director?

25. Can a board exclude a director from any executive session meetings?

26. Who can remove an officer from his or her office?

27. If an officer is removed from the office, is she still a director?

28. Fill in the blanks: _____ is what a board "can" do;
_____ is what a board "must" do.

29. A director has a good friend who provides landscape service for his personal business. At a board meeting, the director recommends the association hire his friend because he does great work at a great price.
    a. Is that a conflict of interest?
    b. Where would you look to find the answer?

30. If an association's declaration was recorded prior to December 31, 2014, does the association have authority to regulate roadways within a non-gated community where the ownership of the roadways have been dedicated to or held by a government entity?

31. When a home is sold in a community, how many days after receiving written request does the association have to provide the information?

32. What risk does the association assume if the required information in question 31 is not provided to an escrow agent within the ten day period?

33. What planned community law governs the re-sale of units?

34. Where do you look in order to find what parliamentary procedure your association uses?

35. What are some rules of decorum for meetings?

36. What are six steps to a motion?

37. What does a "second" mean?

38. Must the person making the second be in favor of the motion?

39. What does it mean to "Lay on the Table"?

40. What is to "Postpone Indefinitely"?

41. What is to "Postpone to a Certain Time"?

42. What is a "Main Motion" and when can it be introduced?

43. Can the maker of a motion withdraw her motion?

44. Name the thirteen motions in their order of precedence.

45. The board discusses an issue for fifteen minutes. When a motion is made regarding the issue, no one seconds it. The chairman says the motion died because there was no second. Is that correct?

46. What information may an association demand from an owner regarding a tenant?

47. Does an association have the right to see the tenant's lease and credit report?

48. For what reason can an association foreclose on a member's home?

49. At what point does that ability get triggered?

50. During what time period can an association prohibit a political sign?

51. Can an association prohibit children from playing on a roadway that is under the jurisdiction of an association if the posted speed limit is twenty-five miles an hour?

52. Name some of the duties of a board of directors.

53. Who can call a special board meeting?

54. How much notice must be provided?

Thank you for purchasing and reading this study guide. I wish you all the best in your interactions with your HOA, whether as a Director on the Board of Directors, or as a homeowner. Please take a couple of minutes and leave a book review on Amazon.

Please Like our Facebook page:
https://www.facebook.com/HOAboards/

Visit the HOA Boards blog: http://HOAboards.net

Captain Bill Travis's other book:
**"Pan Am Captain, Aiming High"**
Available on Amazon.com and can be ordered through all bookstores.

Printed in the USA
CPSIA information can be obtained
at www.ICGtesting.com
LVHW020826230224
772590LV00041B/757